God's Way and Marriage

Its Origin, Covenant, Revelation, Insight, Reasons for it and its Success

AUDREY L. DICKEY, PH.D.

Kingdom Advance Publishing
P. O. Box 48288
Los Angeles, California 90048
877.333.5075

robertandaudreydickeyministries.org

Printed in the United States of America

ISBN: 978-0-9997611-3-7

Library of Congress Control Number: 2017919834
Kingdom Advance Publishing, Los Angeles, CA

Christian Life / Marriage

DEDICATION

I thank God for my loving and dear parents: the late *Mr. and Mrs. Henry W. and Lillian C. Jones.* They were an inspiration and true examples of Godly, loving parents who gifted each and every one of their ten children with the love they shared for each other.

The love they shared lasted fifty-eight years, as husband and wife, companions and best friends, until my father went to heaven and my mother followed nine and a half years later. Together once again, this time for eternity!

CONTENTS

FORWARD

After nearly 25 years of marriage to this apostle, prophet, teacher, pastor and evangelist, I am truly amazed at the great insight, wisdom and discernment that God has given Dr. Audrey regarding Godly relationships, especially marriage.

In this manuscript involving seven chapters dealing with the subject of marriage she discusses major concerns in each on the theme. She explains each chapter topic with such insight, wisdom and clarity; thoroughly interweaving scripture with spiritual understanding and practical applicability.

She first, gives an exegesis of God creating marriage in the Garden and what affected it during the Fall. Then she carefully takes us through the protocol of God's marriage covenant which is illustrated with God's marriage to Israel; the early Jewish marriage; then with the marriage of Christ and the Church; and finally of today's marriage between a man and a woman.

Deftly, she deals with such subjects as: reasons for marriage, giving several reasons and blessings; love as the essence of marriage, pointing to God as the central ingredient of that love; how two can become one in marriage; and then she gives a complete exegesis of covenants to increase our understanding of the importance of the marriage covenant itself.

As if this were not enough, she then gives very sound suggestions on how to have a strong, successful marriage in this age of divorce being as prevalent as marriage.

I recommend that everyone read this treatise on marriage whether you are married or wanting information on what to look for, for those looking or expecting from God to find his or her lifelong partner. After reading this presentation, you will have confidence and a good understanding about what it takes to have a strong, successful marriage.

"Find a good spouse, you find a good life – and even more; the favor of God"
Proverbs 18:22, The Message Bible

Robert L. Dickey, PhD
Co-Founder of Christian Love Glory International Center
Home of Christian Love Fellowship Church, Inc.
And Marketplace Business in Los Angeles, California

INTRODUCTION

The truth is marriage can be wonderful when you function in it *God's Way.*

The restoration of marriage is here! The marriage that God gave is being restored and will continuously move forward in strength. It will once again be in its sacred position. In the place where the living God placed it when He created it at the conception of mankind.

He is taking marriage back to its roots and original intent. Therefore, inside these pages you will discover the marriage God designed and intended along with scriptures for personal study. Beginning from the time a couple meets, to becoming engaged (betrothal stage) and through the preparation for the wedding. Followed by details of how to become one and live together in the union of marriage.

This resource will bring clarity, healing, understanding, revelation, and deliverance to marriages. You will find answers, instructions, history and the protocol for marriage from historical times until today.

Reasons for marriage are also shared. Furthermore, this information will impart to a single person guidance and preparation for their future spouse.

Embedded within the sphere of marriage are components that will assist a couple and cause their marriage to flourish. The following list are only a few of those components: true love, the anointing power of God, wisdom, peace, commitment, respect, honor, sharing, security, honesty, selflessness, friendship, companionship, comfort, support and protection.

Best of all, each married couple can discover the reason and purpose for their marriage. As they function in marriage the way God intended, revelation and vision (their assignment) as a couple, will become clear as God reveals the true purpose of why they are married and what they are to accomplish.

Contrary to what most believe, a couple should not decide to marry only to have a home and family and live happily ever after. That may be a part of the foundation but it certainly is not the fullness of why two people should marry. Marriage is much more than that. It has a deeper meaning, especially for those couples that are in God ordained marriages.

A God ordained marriage consists of a couple's awareness that they are with the person God chose for them to share their life with. The Lord knows the purpose of each life and one way He chooses a partner for another, is by the mission or vision they have together. Whether they are aware of their future assignment or not at the time of marriage is irrelevant. God will reveal it at the appointed time.

Nothing is by chance or accident. God's will is His plan and purpose and He always has a plan. His plan is designed to work for our good, Jeremiah 29:11. His plan is greater than what we can see with our natural eyes. We will need to discover His plan with our heart (spiritual eyes and understanding).

The Lord is "the same yesterday, today, and forever," Hebrews 13:8 NKJV. He does not change. He is the Most High God. If we decide to follow, yield to His will, He will not disappoint but do exceedingly, abundantly above all that we could ask or imagine, Ephesians 3:20.

In addition, to *Become One* (like-minded) with the right one will help build, maintain and preserve the precious gift of marriage. During the first few years of marriage this seems to be one of the most difficult things for many couples to achieve. It is during this process of becoming one that many give up, separate and/or divorce.

Learn how to overcome this hurdle as we discuss how to 'Become One' with your spouse. To be on one accord, living in agreement which brings contentment and peace is crucial for a marriage. Thus, when functioning God's way, one's marriage will not only survive it will thrive in times when so many outside forces are fighting against this sacred covenant to rip it apart.

Furthermore, included are suggestions for a strong, stable and successful marriage. These suggestions will give you the missing elements that will put a boring, selfish or non-committed marriage on track to becoming a loving, thoughtful, relationship both partners can truly embrace. Thus, opening the door for increase, peace, joy and so much more.

Last but certainly not least, God is releasing His glory to the earth like mankind has never seen before. With His glory He will transition those in the Kingdom of God for the better! They will experience a refreshing and a new beginning as God's glory transforms the earth.

When you live for His glory (His tangible presence), everything in your life will prosper, including your marriage!

Chapter 1
The Origin of Marriage

Understanding the origin of Marriage will give you an appreciation and an awareness of what marriage really is, why it is important and not to be taken lightly. The following pages display divine revelation coupled with information that will build a strong and powerful foundation concerning marriage. Therefore, when it is time for your marriage to take a stand against opposition or face challenges it will be able to withstand the test and win. *That means your marriage will not only survive it will thrive.*

God is the Creator. To create is always an act of God, whether it is a spiritual creation or a natural creation. Thus, "God has both the sovereign power and the purposive intelligence to bring forth creation in an orderly, designed fashion, so that it is pleasing to Him."

Before the Beginning You were and there is no End in You. You always were and You always will be! Revelation 22:13 says, *"I am the Alpha and the Omega, the First and the Last (the Before all and the End of all)."* He is the Almighty, the Ruler of all, Revelation 1:8.

The Word of God (Jesus; Holy Bible; Torah), the effective tool or instrument God uses to confirm creating, blessing or chastising... *"God created through His Word.* In creating, God brought things into existence out of nothingness. He did not take previously existing matter and transform it into new kinds of material objects. He ended with the whole of existence brought into being out of His powerful Word."[1] (Genesis 1:3 to 2:25.)

From Him All Things Were Created, Romans 11:36 says,

> For from Him and through Him and to Him are all things. [For all things originate with Him and come from Him; all things live through Him, and all things center in and tend to consummate and to end in Him.] To Him be glory forever! Amen (so be it).

In addition, Isaiah 45:12 NIV says,

> *It is I* who made the earth and created mankind on it. My own hands stretched out the heavens; I marshaled their starry hosts. (Emphasis added.)

The word "God" is not a name, it is a title. A title the Creator gave Himself. It means *Self-Existing One*. He is the Self-Sufficient One. God needed nothing to exist because He existed within Himself. Therefore, in the beginning of mankind God did not have to reach out and take from any other source because there was none. He was the only One existing.

So out of Himself He brought forth the heavens and the earth. Out of Himself He brought forth mankind, the animals and all that is in the earth. He knows what is inside of Him, therefore, He knows what it is purposed for once He manifests it.

Whoever Creates a Thing Knows what the *True Purpose* it was Created for, Genesis 1:1 says,

In the Beginning God (prepared, formed, fashioned and) created the heavens and the earth.

Psalm 19:1 NLT says,

The heavens tell of the glory of God. The skies display His marvelous craftsmanship.

Colossians 1:16 says,

For it was in Him that all things were created, in heaven and on earth, things seen and things unseen, whether thrones, dominions, rulers, or authorities; all things were created *and* exist through Him [by His service, intervention] and in *and* for Him.

Revelation 4:11 says,

> Worthy are You, our Lord and God, to receive the glory and the honor and dominion, for You created *all things;* by Your will they were [brought into being] and were created.

Even though He is One God, within Him relationships exist such as the Father, Son and Holy Spirit. In Genesis 1:1 **He is Elohim** – God our Sovereign, Mighty Creator! Elohim is Hebrew and it means God is in plural form. He is One God yet He is multidimensional in His nature. He demonstrates this in Genesis 1:26 when He said "Let Us..." When He made mankind in His image and likeness He again, brought forth from Himself. Therefore, God has within Himself both the masculine and the feminine, the male and female. He was carrying "mankind" within Himself to be released at the appointed time in His likeness!

Genesis 1:26-28 tells us,

> God said, **Let Us [Father, Son, and Holy Spirit]** make mankind in Our image, after Our likeness, and let them have complete authority over the fish of the sea, the birds of the air, the [tame] beasts, and over all of the earth, and over everything that creeps upon the earth. So God created man in His own image, in

the image *and* likeness of God *He created him; male and female He created them. And God blessed them* and said to them, Be fruitful, multiply, and fill the earth, and subdue it [using all its vast resources in the service of God and man]; and have dominion over the fish of the sea, the birds of the air, and over every living creature that moves upon the earth. (Emphasis added.)

Thus, God created mankind but why in His image? The Word of God says in I John 4:16, "...God is Love." The Word does not say God only has love or that He only expresses love, or He just gives love, it says *He is Love.* Because God is Love He chose not to exist by Himself so "He created him; male and female" to have someone to love. A bride (the bride of Christ the Messiah, Jew and Gentile in Messiah, Eph. 2:14-16) was created for Messiah to dwell with on the earth. Thus, He created mankind, making them in His own image.

However, *He not only created them to love and have a bride but also to bless and be a part of their marriage and family. In addition, He also created them to share His rulership and in His government.*

Thus, mankind was given dominion, to govern to keep and maintain the earth's beauty, glory and the order set in the earth by God Himself. This all meant man would even govern and rule the fallen cherub angel, Lucifer. After he was removed from heaven and sent to the earth, his name was changed to Satan, the Devil in addition to other titles and names given to him, Isaiah 14:12-15. He is the number one enemy or adversary of mankind over whom mankind was given dominion, Luke 10:18-19.

We are not to live in fear of him but to keep him under our feet where God placed him. Therefore, this resource on marriage will also include information and revelation that will include some spiritual warfare strategies for the handling of our marriage and home.

We must understand that even though God created Adam which means man or mankind (male and female) and desires they have an abundant and prosperous life (See *God's Way and Finances)* we have an enemy who was on the earth when *mankind* was created. Adam (male and female) was placed in a position of rulership to govern and have dominion over the earth, Gen. 1:26-27. (See *God's Way and Spiritual Warfare.)*

As long as we remain close to our Creator He will continue to impart wisdom, strategies, protection, provision, guidance, strength, joy and whatever else we need to receive and live the life He destined for our marriage from the beginning.

When God created mankind, both of them were present in one physical body and **they were both named Adam** which in Hebrew means "man, mankind, or natural man."

Genesis 5:2 tells us,

> He created them male and female and
> blessed them and named them [both]
> Adam [Man] at the time they were
> created.

**The Lord's creation of mankind was a
"male" man and a "female" man** whom He created,
blessed and spoke to from the beginning. Their union
created the first marriage covenant. The male and
female also mean, "It takes two to make one."

Thereby God was expressing that He created all
of mankind when He made both the male and female
(mankind: two different genders, each gender having a
spirit, soul and body). Furthermore, the "female"
Adam was called "wo-man" by the "male" Adam in
Genesis 2:23 because she was taken out of a man.
"The man called his wife's name Eve [Life Spring]
because she was the mother of all the living" Genesis
3:20.

When God first spoke to His creation, the
"male" man was the only one present before Him in a
physical human body, Genesis 1:26-27. However, the
"female" was very much present but as a *hidden
support.*

In the case of the *female* man the shape of her
body at the time was not a great concern to Father God
because God knew they were both before Him and
they both could hear Him.

God spoke to *them* as seen in scripture, Genesis 1:28. So why would His Holy Bible say God spoke to *them* when it was very clear in the natural the only one standing before God in human form was the "male" Adam? God made mankind in His image and likeness.

In John 4:24 it says, "God is a Spirit (a spiritual Being) ..." **The true person is a spiritual being that lives in a physical body that possesses a soul which is comprised of their mind, will and emotions.** Mankind is part *spirt, soul and body,* I Thess. 5:23.

Therefore, the Lord was communicating with both of their *spirits* as He is a Spiritual Being Himself and communicates with human beings from His Holy Spirit to their spirit man, as He does to this day.

Furthermore, *His Holy Spirit will communicate with a person's spirit man regardless of the type of body it is occupying* at the time. And whether the body is whole or deformed, well or sick, black, white, red, yellow or brown, tall or short, bald, ugly or beautiful it really does not matter.

Even though He loves and appreciates you because He is love and created all of mankind, He does not and will not communicate with a person's body. The body itself does not carry life but it carries the blood with the spirit of life in it. God only communicates with a person's spirit because it is where the life is located. The only thing that matters here is the condition of our spiritual heart, it is where our spirit man lives inside of us.

The fact is, the "female" Adam lived in a rib or the "male" man's side temporarily before God made or formed her human body. In Hebrew Tzela' means *rib* and Tzad means *side*. A side can be seen as *a hidden support*. For example: a wall, leaves, boards and so forth according to Strong's Concordance. She was alive and could hear simply because the true person is a "spiritual being" and is made in the image of God. To demonstrate how this could be, we will illustrate this point with the beginning of life.

When a child first forms inside of a mother's body, it is in the form of an embryo (the developing human individual from the time of implantation to the end of the eighth week after conception). The Embryonic sack does not resemble the body of a human being, yet it has life in it from the time of conception or it would not continue to grow and develop. *The spirit is life and the life is in the blood. The spirit of the baby was in the embryonic sack as the spirit of the woman was in the rib or the man's side.*

When God brought them both forth at the same time He demonstrated He had completed bringing forth mankind. When God made man out of dust, fully grown, surely, He could place a spirit in the *male* Adam's rib until the appointed time to form a second human body. Again, the beginning stages of the human body before it was formed and how it was formed is not the important thing because the person is a spirit that simply lives in a body and has a soul.

Furthermore, I Corinthians 11:12 also confirms mankind ultimately comes from God as it says, "For as woman was made from man, even so man is also born of woman; and all [whether male or female go forth] from God [as their Author]."

God sees the heart in people (mankind) and He chooses to be in fellowship with human beings but when the motives and heart is wicked, evil, full of doubt and fear they are unable to communicate with Him. When their heart is righteous and pure and they are sensitive to Him they will be able to hear Him clearly when He speaks. (See *God's Way and Knowing the King* for additional revelation of having a personal relationship with a True and Living God.)

Also realize, after saying the marriage vows a married couple has ***supernaturally become one in the spirit*** in the sight of God. Therefore, when He speaks to the husband or wife He is speaking to the plan He has that will affect both of their lives. This is one very important reason why a husband and his wife should discuss things and come in agreement before a final decision has been made. In order to be successful, the decisions that need to be made and things that need to be accomplished should be made as individuals, their marriage and the family in alignment with the will of God.

God gave them dominion and instructions together because they were called to be spiritual partners as well. In Him the male and female stand on equal ground each having an equal responsibility to follow His instructions (commands) and be obedient to His will and not their own. Therein, the Lord has given the male and female authority over the earth, *not to take dominion over each other* but rather to take dominion over living creatures, the environment and their circumstances.

In Genesis 1:26 the Amplified Bible as seen above states God the Father made a decision with the Son of God and Holy Spirit to make mankind in their image and give them complete authority on the earth.

In Genesis, it gives an account of how God brought "mankind" into being in the body of the "male" Adam from the dust of the ground. Ground in Hebrew is "Adamah." Notice the Lord breathed into the "male" Adam's nostrils and gave them (for the female Adam was inside of him) life! This was the first union of heaven with earth. God breathed His life, nature and spirit into dust. Therefore, mankind is on earth but not from earth because he was to be a portal between heaven and earth. An open door so God had access to mankind and mankind had access to God in heaven.

Genesis 2:7 says,

> Then the Lord formed man from the dust of the ground and **breathed into his nostrils** the breath or spirit of life, and man became a living being. (Emphasis added.)

Ecclesiastes 12:7 says,

> Then shall the dust [out of which God
> made man's body] return to the earth as
> it was, and the spirit shall return to God
> Who gave it.

God had given the male Adam a home, work
and instructions on how to live before He formed the
female Adam to join him Genesis 2:15-17. He was
given work by God to tend, guard and keep the Garden
of Eden. Which He meant for His creation to cultivate,
prosper and multiply that which was planted in the
Garden.

The male Adam had already named the animals
and had seen them with their partners. And I am sure
he could not help but wonder, why he does not have a
partner who was suitable for him to share his life with,
Genesis 2:19-20.

Adam had a personal relationship with God and
I believe God gave Adam a vision to spread His glory,
goodness and wealth throughout the world. **But Adam
needed a partner to love, to share with, to bring
forth children and for help with the vision God
placed in his heart.**

God said from the beginning they were to be
fruitful, multiply, fill the earth, subdue it and have
dominion over it and all that was living in it, Genesis
1:28. Therefore, Adam desired a partner, a wife
because he was made in God's image which came with
the need and desire to love someone else.

God showed him the difference in being alone compared to how it would be to be in a relationship. To be in a relationship with someone he could relate to, love and share his life with. A companion that was adaptable and complementary to himself.

In the same chapter God answers Adam's desire and brings the woman forth in human form.

Genesis 2:21-22 tells us,

> And the Lord God created a deep sleep to fall upon Adam; and while he slept, **He took one of his ribs *or* a part of his side** and closed up the [place with] flesh. And the rib *or* part of his side which the Lord God had taken from the man *He built up and made into a woman*, and He brought her to the man. (Emphasis added.)

With this, the first marriage covenant took place. Notice also, *when the Lord built the woman He did not have to breathe into her nostrils the breath or spirit of life for her to become a living being because she was already alive* inside of the "male" Adam waiting for the appointed time to have a physical body of her own. God said He built or made her and then brought her to the man Adam.

I once heard a Bishop give a beautiful illustration regarding a woman being formed from a man's rib and he said, *"She was taken from under his arm for protection, by his side for fellowship and next to his heart for love.*"

She was built from the man's side to stand with him, side by side, as husband and wife in partnership ready to complete their vision and assignment together as they walked in authority. In order for them to take dominion on the earth Father God along with God the Son and God the Holy Spirit (One God, three different manifestations of His personality as He is Three in One) agreed upon from mankind's conception, Genesis 1:26, Deuteronomy 6:4, John 1:1.

Genesis 2:23, 25 tells us,

> Then Adam said, This [creature] is now bone of my bones and flesh of my flesh; she shall be called Woman, because she was taken out of a man... And the man and his wife were both naked and were not embarrassed *or* ashamed in each other's presence.

In this covenant God Himself was a part of the union thereby making marriage a covenant between a man, a woman and God Himself. (See the *Chapter Six* regarding the Marriage Covenant for additional information and revelation).

Father God brought the woman to the man as a loving earthly father would escort his daughter down the aisle to be wed. God brings a man who is searching for a wife, *the right wife.* He brings the best that that particular husband needs and desires. Proverbs 18:22 says "He who finds a [true] wife finds a good thing and obtains favor from the Lord."

One of the things God says a married woman is, is a helper meet (help meet; helpmate). She is someone who is suitable for her husband, adapted, and complementary to her mate, Genesis 2:20. She is one who is capable and equipped and is sent by God with wisdom, knowledge, gifts and skills to assist her husband. She is her husband's confidante, encourager, spiritual partner, an inward strength and comforter; she is his "helper." She is sent by God to help him fulfill his purpose and vision.

I like to say, as a helper, she is in excellent company because one of the names or attributes of Holy Spirit is "Helper" Hebrews 13:6 and John 16:7. In Psalm 121:2 it says, "My help comes from the Lord, Who made heaven and earth." Here He describes Himself as a "Helper" as well. However, God in all His power was still humble (Phil. 2:8-9) enough to be called a *Helper* and has placed *a wife* in a similar position on earth in the most important institution known to mankind, *"Marriage."*

With wisdom and knowledge ladies, you are equipped as a *helper* to use your God-given skills for daily tasks which are *not limited* to running the affairs of your household. A woman's desire to support her husband is simply a manifestation of her God-given nature as a helpmate. Women were created with a natural need to secure, protect, correct and to give advice. (See *God's Way and Family* for more details about a wife's role and functions.)

According to the Word of God, the *first family* was birthed through the union of a marriage. *Marriage takes precedence over child parent* ties as illustrated by what God chose to create first. He could have created an entire "family" rather than a man and a woman first but *He chose to start with a marriage* and then add to the structure of His creation.

Technically, a marriage without children is a "child-free family." His ways and thoughts are always higher than ours, Isaiah 55:8-9. He has a better plan and ultimately whatever God does is done for the good and benefit of mankind, Genesis 2:21-25; Jeremiah 29:11.

The rendering of several words and phrases in the Hebrew and Greek referring to marriage are as follows: to be "master;" to "take," that is a wife; to "magnify" or "lift up" a woman; to "contract;" to "dwell together;" to "perform the duty of brother;" and to "become," that is the wife of one. *In all the Hebrew Scriptures, there is no single word for the estate of marriage or to express the abstract idea of wedlock* [2] paraphrased.

The revelation of both male and female being created together and how they fulfill purpose in their marriage is not intended to put one gender down or the other up. Neither gender is to be exalted and neither is depreciated. But both are meant to complement (complete) the other by recognizing their differences and the purpose for those differences then respecting, honoring and appreciating the differences.

Restoration of the Original Position and Plan of God

We have established God is the Creator, according to His Holy Scriptures, and the evidence is His creation and all that is in it. In addition, He gave instructions so what He created could fulfill their full purpose and function well on the earth.

As mentioned above in Genesis 1:28, "And God blessed them and said to them, *Be fruitful, multiply, and fill the earth, and subdue it* [using all its vast resources in the service of God and man]; *and have dominion* over the fish of the sea, the birds of the air, and over every living creature that moves upon the earth." However, we are all aware *Adam and Eve were deceived and lost their authority and dominion to the adversary,* Satan in Genesis 3:1-7.

Once that took place both of their positions in the spiritual realm, their home and roles in life changed, Genesis 3:14-24. **The woman was removed from being a valid married spouse** to being someone her husband ruled over. Over the years the woman became an afterthought; created solely for a man's use and pleasure; and seen as his property instead of a full functioning partner in matrimony.

As a result of the fall women had very little say or rights. In most countries women could not own property, own businesses or even file for a divorce if the need arose. Women became restricted, limited and most of their liberties were removed. And verse 16 says, "I will greatly multiply your grief *and* your suffering in pregnancy *and* the pangs of childbearing; with spasms of distress you will bring forth children."

Because of the fall the "male" man suffered as well. The Word says in verse 17-19 "...the ground is under a curse because of you; in sorrow and toil shall you eat [of the fruits] of it all the days of your life..." He lost his home in the Garden of Eden, his position, spiritual insight, his relationship and the favor he once had with Almighty God.

To keep the male and female down and out of the cycle of life God placed them in, the enemy uses distractions and circumstances to wear couples out so they can forfeit their blessed marriage, blessings, ministries, businesses and future. This is really the greatest reason for the increase in divorce. *But couples can fight back!* (See *Chapter Seven*, Suggestions for a Strong, Successful Marriage.)

The enemy works hard at causing you to lose focus, getting you off track and then causing suffering because of it. He wants your identity masked to keep the truth from being known, that if you are a child of *The King of kings* you are alive, free and empowered by Holy Spirit.

He is the Divine Third Person of the Trinity, and will stand firm against any enemy, fight victoriously and win every battle! When you are in a state of resting in Him, fully trusting God, He fights your enemies for you.

My Point is this, *God gave these two people, a husband and his wife, dominion together to rule* but because of their fallen state they did not operate in any real power against circumstances that occurred in their marriage or life.

But my God has also given a way of escape and He makes all things new! When Jesus paid the price for our sins it reconciled mankind back to Father God. It brought the male and female back to mankind's original state of being. This placed them back into position, restoring them to where they are supposed to be. The Bible says they can shed the old and become a "new creature" or a "new man" in Christ Messiah, 2 Cor. 5:17; Eph. 2:14.

Colossians 3:1-17 and See Verses 1, 3, 9, 10, 11 below,

> IF THEN you have been raised with Christ [to a new life, thus sharing His resurrection from the dead], aim at *and* seek the [rich, eternal treasures] that are above, where Christ is, seated at the right hand of God. **(3)** For [as far as this world is concerned] you have died, and your

[new, real] life is hidden with Christ in God... **(9)** Do not lie to one another, for you have stripped off the old (unregenerate) self with its evil practices, **(10)**And have clothed yourselves with the new [spiritual self], which is [ever in the process of being] renewed *and* remolded into [fuller and more perfect knowledge upon] knowledge after the image (the likeness) of Him Who created it... **(11)** ...Christ is all and in all [everything and everywhere, to all men, without distinction of person] ..." [Genesis 1:26].

It is time for the male and female to once again have the authority that was given to them in the Garden of Eden. Where the original plan of God, was removed when they were deceived, sinned and fell.

Luke 10:19 Reveals Our Authority in the Earth,

Behold! I have given you authority *and* power to trample upon serpents and scorpions, and [physical and mental strength and ability] over all the power that the enemy [possesses]; and nothing shall in any way harm you.

When God gave dominion to both of them, He gave the "male" man the helpmeet he needed. This is one reason why God sends a spouse with the same vision or a heart for a similar purpose that is in God's will (His plan and purpose).

When a male marries a female, they have supernaturally become one in the spirit in the eyes of God. When they receive the gift of salvation which can be offered because of the price Jesus paid at the cross, then when this couple comes in agreement *their prayers will be the most powerful prayers on the face of the earth.* Their decrees will see results and they will experience manifestations of answered prayers.

The Word says whosoever receives Messiah Jesus as their Lord and Savior shall be saved and they become a new man (mankind) which brings about restoration from the fall. The Believer also receives power and authority in His name, Matthew 28:18.

As men and women operate in their authority in Christ Messiah, they will recapture the spoils that were taken illegally by the adversary and his evil followers (spiritual and in the natural). These spoils will include but are not limited to reconciliation in family, friend and business relationships, health restored, property restored, finances increased, children blessed, and so on, Luke 10:19; Matthew 16:19; Isaiah 54:17 and Psalms 91:10-11; Prov. 6:31; 2 Corinthians 9:8.

During the End-Times the Lord is restoring the female (wo-man) back to her original state, a position God placed her in from the beginning. Since the fall and over many centuries, her authority has been misplaced or removed. The adversary using evil devices, influences and spirits have continuously worked through people throughout the ages to remove the female from God's original plan.

Therefore, by restoring her to a position of authority, when the male and female agree upon a matter they will operate in power with full authority in Christ and take dominion as promised. **This would be the greater reason for the "female" man having been created.** For them to come in agreement and release a greater power when they exercise their authority and take dominion. *The two of them taking dominion will complete one of God's purposes for mankind being on the face of this earth in addition to giving Him Praise and displaying His Glory!*

The Word of God says, one will put a thousand to flight and two ten thousand giving the two of them the ability to take back what was stolen. At the same time, it will defeat the enemy in their lives, Deut. 32:20.

God is Restoring Clarity to the Female's Identity in this Season of Restoration

Restoration has already begun in the spirit and is now manifesting in the natural realm at an accelerated pace. However, *women need to know their identity so they can flow with the Spirit of God.* The enemy will attempt to magnify a woman's insecurities and devalue her strengths which can cause her to doubt what God says about her and what He has given her. It will also dominate how she sees herself, disabling and attempting to disarm her from fighting back and being who God really created her to be in this life.

Our true identity whether we are male or female begins when our spirit man comes "alive" and we are adopted into God's family. Once Born-again (anew, from above; saved), we receive the very life, heart and nature of God, John 3:3.

As our Spirit man grows (through fellowship with God by spending time in prayer; reading His Word and learning of His ways) our soul is transformed. Because of this our soul (mind, will and emotions) will align with our spirit so we can become what God determined and intended for us to be. In other words, we receive our call-in life and fulfill our purpose.

Romans 12:2 says,

> Do not be conformed to this world (this age), [fashioned after and adapted to its external, superficial customs], but be transformed (changed) by the [entire] renewal of your mind [by its new ideals and its new attitude], so that you may prove [for yourselves] what is the good and acceptable and perfect will of God, even the thing which is good and acceptable and perfect [in His sight for you].

Remember, the Father of glory has *granted you the "spirit of wisdom and revelation [of insight into mysteries and secrets]* in the [deep and intimate] knowledge of Him ... so that you can know *and* understand (discern and comprehend) the hope to which He has called you,... And [so that you can know and understand] what is the immeasurable *and* unlimited *and* surpassing greatness of His power in *and* for you who believe, as demonstrated in the working of His mighty strength," Eph.1:17-19. **Bottom line, you must know who you are in Christ.** We are the children of Light... we are able through Christ to produce the fruit of the Light, Eph. 5:8-9.

We cannot stress how important it is *to know who you are and what you are called to do and where you are supposed to be.* Otherwise the lies of the enemy come and if you entertain the lies you will develop a stronghold and you will not feel equipped or entitled to stand firm against the enemy.

This is also what happens when people who are in guilt and condemnation find it difficult to move forward with strong faith. They will need prayer to destroy the stronghold and, in the future, not entertain the lies of the enemy, the vain imaginations and allow them to hinder or stop them. Instead cast them down and out of our lives!

2 Corinthians 10:3-5 NIV tells us,

> For though we live in the world, we do not wage war as the world does. The weapons we fight with are not the

weapons of the world. On the contrary, they have divine power to demolish strongholds. We demolish arguments and every pretension that sets itself up against the knowledge of God, and we take captive every thought to make it obedient to Christ.

Our true identity is linked to the invisible world, not to the natural. Some never experience their true identity. Don't choose to go through life saying, "I just want a regular practical life." All that means is you want to be accepted and conform to the world's standard. It could also mean you have grown weary in well doing and no longer choose to pursue your dreams or purpose in life.

You can discover your identity by noticing how the Lord is transforming you by the Spirit of God. This would involve certain tests and/or circumstances or a path where you will grow and be strengthened in your character. It may also be things are revealed to you that possibly need to be confronted or resolved.

In any event, each person's path is different. Pay attention to what God is doing in your life and work/flow with the Holy Spirit. As you reach out to Father God in prayer He will have your Helper (Holy Spirit) supernaturally strengthen you. He will enable you by His grace to finish what He began in you as you continue to grow spiritually. Also, Satan knows what has been written by God about women and it is another reason why women are fought so viciously by the enemy, Ephesians 6:12.

It is time to become who we as women were meant to be by the Spirit of God. It is time to take off the cloak of heaviness and put on our garment of praise.

It is time for women to know their true identity and walk in it. God is raising up women in this hour not to usurp, compete or overpower a man but *to come alongside him.* This will increase the power and authority God gave both the male and female from the beginning. To be in agreement concerning God's will produces manifestation. When two or more agree, especially a male and a female it shall be done by their Father in heaven, Matthew 18:18-19.

It is time for women to enter into their call in ministry. Some are fivefold (apostles, prophets, evangelists, pastors or teachers) ministers, or in helps ministry, some are praisers, intercessors, warriors, lay ministers and so forth. Many women have administrative gifts and talents, are excellent homemakers, entrepreneurs in the marketplace and professionals (judges, lawyers, doctors, engineers, businesswomen, politicians and so forth).

Whatever God has purposed for your life in a given season, that place is your ministry when you are a child of God. All those Born-again into the Kingdom of God are ministers of reconciliation and called to speak to others about the Gospel of Jesus Christ.

Therefore, in order to receive restoration some of our thinking regarding women and their purpose, function and role, needs to change. So, go back to the beginning of creation and think in a higher dimension as to why God sent a female to this earth.

Many think her only purpose is to be a man's wife or someone's mother. Others believe it is okay for a woman to be a business woman, a professional or the perfect Proverbs 31 Woman. All of the above are honorable. However, God has called, anointed and appointed women from the beginning with a greater responsibility. She and the male *together* as part of the Kingdom of God, with full authority will usher in the glory of God and take dominion in this earth. This process will also help to prepare for the return of the Messiah.

Until women come into their place of authority on the earth, we as a people in the Kingdom of God are not going to see the fullness of the fruitfulness God has for His Church. Neither will we see the fullness of Kingdom dominion in the earth. *Male and female both must be in their place to see the fullness. Therefore, it is time for women to emerge.*

Please recall **Esther's identity was hidden,** Esther 2:10 and the fact women began on this earth as a hidden support inside of a "male" man in the form of a rib. **A woman's true identity has been hidden.** God brought Esther out of hiding in time to save a nation of Jewish people. *God is bringing the "woman" out of hiding into position for such a time as this!* She is to take dominion alongside the "male" man, save the lost and demonstrate the light of *God's Glory* has come to this earth!

God is Mindful of Man, Psalm 8:3-9 says,

When I view *and* consider Your heavens, the work of Your fingers, the moon and the stars, which You have ordained *and* established, What is man (the word mankind is used in the NIV) that You are mindful of him, and the son of [earthborn] man that You care for him? Yet You have made him but a little lower than God [or heavenly beings], and You have crowned him with glory and honor. You made him to have dominion over the works of Your hands; You have put all things under his feet: All sheep and oxen, yes, and the beasts of the field, the birds of the air, and the fish of the sea, *and* whatever passes along the paths of the seas. O Lord, our Lord, how excellent (majestic and glorious) is Your name in all the earth!

Chapter 2

Marriage Protocol: Early to Modern Times

Marriage on earth is a type and shadow; a pattern if you will, of the *Spiritual Marriage between God and His Bride Israel*. Marriage, as everything else, starts in the spiritual realm *first* and is then manifested into the earthly realm.

God chose Abraham and raised up the nation of Israel. He not only raised up a nation, *God said He would be married to this nation and to this people.*

Isaiah 54:5-6 tells us,

> For your Maker is your Husband -- the Lord of hosts is His name -- and the Holy One of Israel is your Redeemer; the God of the whole earth He is called. For the Lord has called you like a woman forsaken, grieved in spirit, and heartsore even a wife [wooed and won] in youth...

Isaiah 62:5 NIV tells us,

> For as a young man marries a young woman, so will your Builder marry you; as a bridegroom rejoices over his bride, so will your God rejoice over you.

The Marriage Protocol Between God and Israel

God has a covenant with Israel and it continues to this day. Now we will describe how **God married Israel.** We will also show why protocol or etiquette still has a great influence on marriages today.

First there was the *covenant (contract) from the Lord to Israel,* Exodus 24:1-7. This contract was called the Torah, the Hebrew Bible. It usually refers to the first five books of the Bible. However, teaching is done from Genesis to Revelation so in essence, Torah covers the entire Bible. Torah, in Hebrew means "teaching" as it gives "instructions" and is also known as the "Law." **Second,** Israel *agreed* to the contract (covenant). **Third,** God told Israel to *sanctify herself,* to be set apart for Him. This was done when they bathed and washed their clothes in order to come into God's presence Exodus 19:10. **Fourth,** God came down upon Mount Sinai [in a cloud] in the sight of all the people (Exo.19:11) and became a *covering* for the people He loves as they went to the Promise Land, Deuteronomy 33:2-3. God was a *covering* to Israel as a man is a covering for his wife. The cloud also represented the huppa or canopy under which the ancient Jewish couple were blessed by the Priest during their wedding ceremony.

We will compare the marriage protocols between the marriages of: God and Israel, the Ancient or Early Jewish Wedding and Marriage, the Marriage procedure between Christ the Messiah and

His Bride the Church (Jew and Gentile in Messiah Jesus, Eph. 2:14-16),[1] and a Marriage today between One Man and One Woman.

The Marriage between God and Israel was the model for the **Ancient Jewish Wedding.** The Jewish wedding originally had fourteen different stages but only the following key points will be briefly discussed.

The *couple met,* usually in the market place while the virgins were shopping. The *man approached her*, they briefly spoke and he took her name and later made arrangements for her to come to his father's house for a *meeting.*

Once the meeting arrangements were prepared, she took her friends with her who waited outside in anticipation of the outcome of this meeting.

To make a long story short, the two of them sat down at a table with the man's father in the center and a *contract* was read to them by the man. The contract listed the obligations of the husband and the wife. It also named the *price* of the bride. The biblical obligation to one another especially for the husband was extensive.

According to the Jewish Bible, the husband must provide for his wife and show respect for her. (Judaism was the first religion that obligated the husband to provide financially for his wife in the event of his death).

Once she *agreed* to the contract and they both signed it, *gifts* were offered to the woman that could include jewelry (Abraham, the father of Isaac, sent his servant with gifts to find his son's wife, Genesis 24:10). They then *sealed* it all with a sip of wine (wine represented it was sealed with a *blood covenant*) given to them by the man's father in a silver cup (silver being the color of *redemption)*.

This process legally binds the man and the woman together because "betrothal vows were as binding as marriage vows even though the couple did not live together until the wedding."[2] *They both understood at this point they were considered to be in the first stage of their marriage, known as the "betrothal stage."* In this stage, the woman is called a "wife."

However, had she accepted and later he changed his mind about the marriage, in order to stop the process, *he would have been required to give her a Bill of Divorce. The marriage had become a binding contract in the betrothal stage.* In the book of Matthew 1:18-21 it is explained, **it was in this stage Jesus' mother was found to be pregnant [through the power] of Holy Spirit.**

Joseph not aware of this considered putting her away with a divorce until he received a visitation from an angel who explained to him that which is conceived in her is of Holy Spirit. The Child would be a Son Who was sent to save His people from their sins and you will call Him Jesus (Yeshua in Hebrew). With that revelation, he continued and later their marriage completed all of the wedding stages.

Today we would refer to this stage as *the engagement period*. However, if she *did not drink of the cup*, then he collected his things and they parted, never to come together again. (The revelation is a mystery that is concealed in the Old Testament and later revealed in the New Testament. That mystery is - if we refuse the invitation to become a part of God's family by rejecting His Son, this would be tantamount to rejecting your invitation to the Marriage Supper of the Lamb with your Bridegroom, Jesus Christ the Messiah, Yeshua HaMashiach, Rev. 19:9.)

If an agreement was reached during the betrothal stage, they did not contact each other; they did not speak, date or do any of those things. She was *sanctifying* herself in preparation for their marriage. The Hebrew term for marriage is Kiddushin, which comes from a root word meaning "holy" and implies sanctification.

Part of this sanctification included wearing a veil across her face in the market place, signifying she is no longer available, she has been *set apart* and belongs to someone else. Wearing the veil was similar in other cultures to wearing an *engagement ring*, signifying you are no longer available and are now set apart and you belong to someone else.

They are now considered *one* for the next twelve months or so. He leaves to go and *prepare a place for her in his father's house*. If he were asked, "When will the big day be?" He would say, "I do not know; only my father knows." *Only the father knew the day* the chamber would be ready (Matthew 24:36) and when the father said it was ready, the groom went for his bride at *night* with others. One in the party would go ahead and shout their coming (I Thessalonians 4:16; I Corinthians 15:52 and Matthew 25:6) and she and her girls would be ready to go.

They stayed ready with a little lamp burning each night while waiting for him to come (Matt. 25:1-13 and Matthew 24:44). Then all were taken to the bridal chamber at his father's house. (Revelation -- notice the correlation with the groom leaving to prepare a place for his bride and what happened after Jesus was resurrected. He walked the earth for forty days and was seen by over five hundred witnesses and then ascended in front of witnesses into the heavens *to go and prepare a place for His bride in His Father's house*, I Cor. 15:6; Matthew 28:1-15.

What was acted out in the Old Testament is truth and mystery was concealed (hidden) and later revealed in the New Testament, I Corinthians 2:7. The Word says, *no one knows the day nor the hour (Matthew 25:13)* but God has given to each man who can discern, the times and season, the season of His return.

All those who are *prepared* and received the sacrifice Jesus made (Luke 23:33) will be with Him as the bride will be with the bridegroom. The young girls are to be prepared with the oil which is a symbol of the Holy Spirit and this instruction shows us it is part of the preparation which is to stay close to the Holy Spirit and be sensitive to His leading especially in these last days!

Now it is time to *complete the process of their marriage*, the *final* stage known as the *"Consummation Stage."* It takes place in the open area under a canopy (called a huppa) which symbolizes the bridal chamber in the presence of God's love that is always protecting the couple. The groom arrives first, then the bride is carried to the bridegroom in a large decorated box like the priest carried the Ark of the Covenant. The groom gives the bride a wedding ring and in the presence of two witnesses, they exchange the traditional wedding vows.

The wedding vows confirm the marriage covenant has taken place. Malachi 2:14 says, "...Yet she is your companion and the wife of your covenant [made by your marriage vows]."

This is then followed by a procession and a big festival which lasts for seven days with family, friends and neighbors; all part of the wedding festival. Revelation: the festival they enjoyed would be equivalent to our celebrating at a wedding reception. Again, this is a type and shadow of a hidden truth or mystery in the Old Testament that is revealed in the New Testament.

The *Consummation or final stage* is one of the steps done during *Passover* which is the first feast given by God to His people and has been enjoyed and celebrated by Jews for centuries and as of the New

Covenant Christian Believers as well, Exodus 12:14-15; I Corinthians 5:7-8. The word *feast* means God set an appointed time for His people to meet with Him.

What is revealed in the final stage? During the Passover Seder (the ceremonial evening meal) with which Passover (Pesach) begins in Jewish as well as many Christian homes (observed by both but may be celebrated differently). In the Jewish home, four cups of red wine are included, each with spiritual significance and blessings. The fourth cup is called the **"Cup of *Consummation*"** which is the cup of the *final thing*.

When Yeshua (Jesus' Hebrew name) an Orthodox Jewish Rabbi observed the *Passover Meal* at the *Last* Supper with His disciples, He did not drink of this cup but set it down. Then He said "I will not drink of the fruit of the vine until the Kingdom of God comes." In other words, I will not drink of it until we are together again, Luke 22:15-18.

The process of redeeming God's people from this world is **hidden** in the stages which lead up to a biblical wedding and marriage and is revealed in the book of Revelation as well as other books of the Bible.

I would also like to add many believe in order to consummate a marriage, to bring it to its final stage, the couple *must* engage in sexual intimacy based on such scriptures as John 3:29 and Song of Solomon 5:1.

Matthew 19:6 says, "So they are no longer two, but one flesh. What therefore God has joined together, let not man put asunder (separate)." The Hebrew and

Greek terms are usually translated "flesh" in regards to the whole human being rather than to merely the sensual or physical aspect of human nature. Becoming one flesh is said to be established through sexual union, but the implications of the term are more than sexual. *This type of union creates a spiritual and psychological interrelationship in which the couple establishes a bond that is more than physical. Therefore, the one flesh union also establishes the bonding of two people because they think in agreement, which is fundamental to a lasting marriage.* God created them to be together to exercise authority in order to take dominion and rule the earth.

So then, **the *final stage to consummate a marriage is the exchange of marriage vows*** because they are "words" and words are spirit and containers of power. There is power in the spoken Word as demonstrated by God Himself Who formed the earth with "Words" Genesis chapter one. The husband and wife are first spiritual beings that dwell in a fleshly body. **When they spoke their vows before God the officiant pronounced them husband and wife.** At that point they *were married and their spirits supernaturally became one in the sight of God.*

Surely sexual intimacy has its part and can be seen as perfecting the final thing but it is not in itself a necessity to finalize the union of matrimony. For instance, a couple who marry after exchanging wedding vows and one of the partners is on their death bed; or another couple who marry just before their spouse is immediately shipped overseas after the ceremony and God forbid he or she may pass away and never return; or a couple where one spouse is incarcerated or a spouse is paralyzed or going into surgery or a woman into delivery.

None of these couples would have had the opportunity to be intimate after the ceremony. Therefore, are they not still considered married? According to God and the laws of the land they are spiritually and legally married because they completed their wedding vows and were pronounced husband and wife.

Spiritually they "became one" in the spirit at the time they repeated their marriage vows. From there they begin to think more alike and are able to come in agreement and over the years grow closer together. They grow closer until their relationship truly becomes connected by their hearts, minds and other character traits they possess individually that will make them *unique as one.*

The following is a breakdown of the four stages: the *covenant, agreement, sanctification and consummation* stages. They are mentioned above in some detail and are preparation that lead to the completion of a biblical wedding and marriage.

These same four stages illustrated below demonstrate **God's procedure, code of behavior or pattern has never changed.** The protocol normally begins with the betrothal stage and ends with the consummation of the marriage. They are as follows: *God* and *His bride Israel*; *a Jewish man* and *a Jewish woman*; *Christ/ Messiah* and *His bride the Church (Jew and Gentile)*; and a *marriage today* between *one man* and *one woman.*

The Marriage Protocol between God and His Bride Israel:

- **First**, God *chose* Israel, arranged a *meeting* with Moses and gave a contract (a *covenant*) and a *gift* of "My Promises" from His Word to Israel;

- **Second**, Israel *agreed* to the contract (covenant);

- **Third**, God told Israel to *sanctify herself* so she bathed and washed her garments;

- **Fourth**, God came down upon Mount Sinai in a cloud and became Israel's *covering* which was the *final stage* of the wedding. (It took place under the Huppa, or canopy, which is a covering where the vows were exchanged).

The Marriage Protocol regarding the Ancient Jewish Wedding between a Jewish man and a Jewish woman:

- **First**, he *chose* her, arranged a *meeting* and gave her a *contract* which included the *price* he would give for a wife;

- **Second**, she *agreed* to the contract and also received *gifts* he prepared for her;

- **Third**, she *sanctified herself* later, when she would bathe surrounded by her virgins;

- **Fourth**, he came to pick her up but no one knew the day or hour because he had to wait until his father said the place that was being prepared was ready. Therefore, she stayed *prepared* in an anticipation of his coming. They were *married* (*final thing*) and *seven blessings were recited to seal* the marriage followed by seven days of *celebration* with family, friends and others.

In the Old Testament (the Tanakh) *Israel is the Bride of Father God.* In the New Testament (B'rit Hadashah) *the same Bride with the addition of Gentiles is called the Church when the people are in Messiah.*

Both the Old and New Covenants illustrate a spiritual marriage between God and His people. The same God marrying His people, Jew and Gentile, one body in Jesus the Messiah, (Yeshua HaMashiach), the One New Man, Eph. 2:14-20.

2 Corinthians 11:2, the Apostle Paul Teaches,

For I am zealous for you with a godly eagerness and a divine jealousy, for I have betrothed you to one Husband, to present you as a chaste virgin to Christ.

Romans 7:4 tells us,

Likewise, my brethren, you have undergone death as to the Law through the [crucified] body of Christ, so that now you may belong to Another, to Him Who was raised from the dead in order that we may bear fruit for God.

The Marriage Protocol between Christ the Messiah and His Bride, the Church (Jew and Gentile in Messiah Jesus), Eph. 2:14-16:

- **First**, Christ *chose* us (we are the church) John 15:16-20. He gave us a *covenant* (**contract**) called the New Testament. He paid a *price* (the cross) for His new bride (1 Co. 7:23). He also gave us spiritual *gifts* of the Holy Spirit; the manifestations of Revelation, Utterance and Power (I Corinthians 12:7-11).

- **Second**, we *agreed* to the covenant (contract) when we accepted Jesus Christ as our Lord and Savior (Romans 10:9-10).

- **Third**, is where part of our *sanctification* is to be baptized in water. The ancient Jewish woman bathed in water as part of sanctifying herself, as did the Israelites who bathed and washed their garments to sanctify themselves. In addition, when we receive the Baptism or the Infilling of the Holy Spirit as well, this will assist us as Believers in living a sanctified lifestyle as we obey the teachings in the Word of God and live by the fruit of the Spirit. He expects us to be consecrated, set apart, having holy behavior, and devout with godly qualities (2 Peter 3:11).

- **Fourth**, Jesus is coming back for His bride (*consummation, final thing*) to receive what He paid the price for and redeem her out of this world. Therefore, He has asked His bride to be *prepared* for His coming, to be without spot or blemish and at peace [in serene confidence, free from fears and agitating passions and moral conflicts] (2 Peter 3:14). Jesus is the **covering** for His bride. This spiritual marriage was **sealed** by the blood that was shed by Jesus (Hebrews 13:20). He has also appropriated and acknowledged us as His by putting His **seal** upon us and giving us His [Holy] Spirit in our hearts... 2 Cor.1:22; Eph. 4:30. The wedding *celebration* will be at the Marriage Supper of the Lamb which will take place in Heaven and will last until we come back to reign with Him (Revelation 19:7-9 KJV). (Emphasis added.)

The tradition of wearing a **"white wedding gown" or dress is biblical.** "White garments represent being in a state of spiritual preparedness, from Ecclesiastes 9:8, Let your garments be always white…" In the book of Revelation 19:7-8 it explains when Jesus returns for His bride she should be arrayed (dressed in especially, splendidly, rich clothing) in fine linen, clean and white.

During the ancient *traditional Jewish wedding, the bride and groom wear white,* symbolizing their sins are forgiven and they will begin married life with a clean slate.

Revelation 19:7-8 says,

Let us rejoice and shout for joy [exulting and triumphant]! Let us celebrate *and* ascribe to Him glory *and* honor, for the marriage of the Lamb [at last] has come, and His bride has prepared herself. *She has been permitted to dress in fine (radiant) linen, dazzling and white* – for the fine linen is (signifies, represents) the righteousness (the upright, just, and godly living, deeds, and conduct, and right standing with God) of the saints (God's holy people). (Emphasis added.)

Christian Believers (Jew and Gentile in Christ is the One New Man, Eph. 2:14-20) are called the Bride of Christ but we are also referred to as the army of the Lord. Revelation 19:14 NKJV says, "And the armies in heaven, clothed in fine linen, white and clean, followed Him on white horses." These were the Believers who returned with Jesus/Yeshua, the King of kings after the Marriage Supper of the Lamb had taken place.

Jesus made a way for us to be one with the Father through His sacrifice on the cross but it was not until the "Marriage Supper of the Lamb" we were completely reunited with Father God and experienced total oneness with Him.

The Marriage Supper of the Lamb is about God restoring us back to Himself, with Himself a Husband and the Believers as His wife, we become one in the flesh (in mind and like thinking) in every way, so we will become one with God in every way. *Jesus the Messiah not only died to save us (Jew and Gentile) but to marry us as well.* (See Dr. Robert L. Dickey's, *The Tri-Tribulation Rapture of the Church,* for information regarding the Rapture of God's church which leads to the Marriage Supper of the Lamb.)

Many cultures use different models from the beginning of a relationship to the day of the wedding. In the United States of America and in many societies around the world, the same biblical pattern is still used today.

Born-again Christian Believers/Saints, God's holy people are not people who do everything right. *For it is not our righteousness, but because of Who is in us makes us holy and righteous,* as it says in 2 Corinthians 5:21 NKJV, "For He made Him who knew no sin *to be* sin for us, that we might become the righteousness of God in Him."

Further Revelation of Why Most Wear White Attire as Tradition for Their Wedding. Scripture, Revelation 19:7-8. [3]

> The white linen bridal gowns we shall wear fulfill a fascinating Bible type that reaches back to the Tabernacle of ancient Israel [Exodus 25-30]. In the Tabernacle, plain white linen symbolized pure righteousness. The linen curtains around the entire Tabernacle – the tent, as it were – were pure white. Therefore, no one could enter through the sides or rear, because no one was perfectly righteous. The door of the Tabernacle was sewn with the colors of Christ – scarlet, purple, and blue threads, indicating sacrifice, royalty, and Heaven. The Israelites entered by the door, so symbolically, they were entering by means of the

Messiah. Jesus said, "I am the door: by Me if any man enter in, he shall be saved, and shall go in and out, and find pasture" (John 10:9). Messianic colors were worn by the priests, and also appeared in the hangings of various courts and in roof coverings.

But now, the Church shall wear white! "...the righteousness of saints." Our appearing in pure white testifies to our final perfection. Paul compared earthly marriage to Christ's marrying the Church, Eph. 5:21-33. Ultimately, we will see the result of the Apostle's exhortation of the infant Church.

After we marry the Lord, we'll reign with Him in His Kingdom on Earth. This is exactly the way the bride returned with her groom after an Israeli marriage – to housing he had arranged for them outside his father's house...

The Wedding Protocol is still an Important enough Event to be Honored Today, a Marriage between One Man and One Woman:

- **First**, the man generally is the one that *chooses* the woman for his wife (Proverbs 18:22). There is a courtship and during the course of it, he may propose marriage (the *betrothal* stage). They may discuss how to handle the obligations/responsibilities for their home and what will be expected of one another. They may also discuss such things as where they will live, careers/work, how many children are expected in this union, what faith will they follow and so forth. This portion would be the oral *contract* of the proposal. He will offer a ring to represent their engagement and this would be his *gift*.

- **Second**, she *agrees* to the proposal (the plan he presented for consideration), which is the **covenant** (**contract**).

- **Third**, she starts to *prepare* herself spiritually, physically, emotionally and makes preparation for the wedding ceremony. Her new attire is set aside (*set apart*) from other garments for this special occasion and she will wear her *engagement ring* (replaces the ancient veil) to further demonstrate that she is set apart and not available. She may even remove herself from old activities, people, places and distractions as preparation for the new thing that is about to happen in her life (these are all forms of *sanctification*).

- **Fourth**, during a traditional biblical wedding ceremony, the groom is positioned near the minister of the Gospel of Jesus Christ, or the Rabbi or the Priest or another officiant. The bride is escorted in on the right side of her father, a place of honor, as he will present her to her husband. (Just like God built up Adam's rib and made it into a woman and brought her to her husband, Gen. 2:22). They will exchange marital vows (*consummate* their marriage) before God (who will validate it) and witnesses. They then will *seal* it with a kiss. The reception (festival, *celebration*) follows next as part of ending the final stage, as well as serving as the beginning of a beautiful marriage. The Holy Spirit is the "Promised *Gift*" and is a *covering* for the marriage as part of the covenant (Acts 1:4). The guests will bring **gifts** which is also biblical. Gifts confirm that a covenant has been made (Genesis 21:30 and Genesis 31:52).

The latter two marriages, one being spiritual and the other in the natural, followed the same pattern as the Old Testament marriages *because the foundation of the New Testament is the Old Testament.* The fact God said He is "the same yesterday, today and forever" still stands, Hebrews 13:8. **What was sacred to God then is sacred to God now!**

The Old Testament conceals within it, events that were to come to pass. These events are revealed in the New Testament explaining why certain things were performed or done a certain way in the Old Testament ("But rather what we are setting forth is a wisdom of God *once hidden* [from the human understanding] and *now revealed* to us by God..." I Corinthians 2:7). (Emphasis added.)

Ancient Jewish customs based on the Word of God were in existence thousands of years before Christianity came into being. The Word of God laid a strong foundation as well as prophetic words that went forth, of which most have already come to pass. Many of the negative events occurring in our society today were spoken forth thousands of years ago and are recorded in the Holy Scriptures. These negative events are affecting our marriages, families, cities, and countries primarily because the basic fundamentals of God's Word for living are being distorted, changed, altered, and ignored, 2 Timothy 3 and Matthew 24:1-44.

Even though there are great attacks against the institution of marriage and the family, you will find God has an army, a plan and a purpose for His people to be victorious. (See *God's Way and Spiritual Warfare*.)

In the Old Testament, issues of life were dealt with mostly by using man's senses, mind and responding to an occasional prophetic word from a prophet. There was also a word or inspired instructions from a priest or king who were empowered with an anointing to lead others if they obeyed God. The people were told in the Old Testament in the book of Jeremiah, a New Covenant would come.

Jeremiah 31:31-33 tells us,

> Behold, the days are coming, says the Lord, when I will make *a new covenant* with the house of Israel…But this is the covenant which I will make with the house of Israel: After those days, says the Lord, I will put My law within them, and *on their hearts will I write it; and I will be their God, and they will be My people.* (Emphasis added.)

The Mosaic Law was never supposed to supersede the Abrahamic Covenant. People were married according to the Mosaic Law, which came after Abraham, until the Messiah Jesus came. Those who received their Messiah, they and all Believers are now married to the Messiah, Jesus Christ, the Anointed One. This speaks of the One New Man where Jew and Gentile are reconciled back to Father God through the Cross. This makes one new quality of humanity out of the two, bringing about covenant restoration, Ephesians 2:14-16.

Galatians 3:7-17 tells us,

> Know *and* understand that it is [really] the people [who live] by faith who are [the true] sons of Abraham…So then, those who are people of faith are blessed *and* made happy *and* favored by God [as partners in fellowship] with the believing

and trusting Abraham. And all who depend on the Law [Who are seeking to be justified by obedience to the Law of rituals] are under a curse *and* doomed to disappointment *and* destruction …But the Law does not rest on faith [does not require faith, has nothing to do with faith], for it itself says, He who does them [the things prescribed by the Law] shall live by them [not by faith]. Christ purchased our freedom [redeeming us] from the curse (doom) of the Law [and its condemnation] by [Himself] becoming a curse for us, for it is written [in the Scriptures], Cursed is everyone who hangs on a tree (is crucified); To the end that through [their receiving] Christ Jesus, the blessing [promised] to Abraham might come upon the Gentiles, so that we through faith might [all] receive [the realization of] the promise of the [Holy] Spirit…

In the New Testament, we were given a new and better Covenant on how to live and handle life's issues that occur day in and day out. Things that are happening in the world to things happening in our homes. Situations where people are growing weary and are tempted to give up on their marriages and other concerns in their lives.

In the New Covenant, Believers are anointed or empowered from the inside by the Spirit of God. This brings an inner strength, fresh revelation and insight with the ability to live or walk by faith trusting the leading of the Holy Spirit. We are also given the ability to daily receive: wisdom, revelation, insight, healing, help, direction and so forth. This is received from the Holy Spirit who is our Teacher, Counselor, Comforter, Helper, Strengthener and Deliverer, amongst other things, John 16:7, 13.

The Holy Spirit is the One who heals us, preserves us, directs our path and delivers us. He is the same One who is the *Gift of the Promise* Father God gave to mankind when He married Israel, Acts 1:4-5. *He dwells in us today when we receive the Father's Son.* He will turn things around as we seek Him, listen for instructions and act on His Word. He is faithful and He will preserve our marriages, families, homes, careers, employment, businesses or whatever we have been empowered and favored with to possess and steward.

The Old Testament and the New Testament are also referred to as the Old Covenant and the New Covenant (see *Chapter six* for additional information on the covenants God has with mankind).

As a final note one of the benefits that come with the New Covenant God gave is eternal life. "When Old Covenant believers died, they were held or preserved in a place the Bible calls Abraham's bosom until the work of redemption was completed, Luke

16:19-31. In this sense of the word, they were saved. However, they did not receive the promise of the new birth until after the Messiah paid the price for man's redemption."

But when Jesus went to the Cross, it all changed. Hebrews 10:14 tells us, "For by a single offering He has forever completely cleansed and perfected those who are consecrated and made holy."

Justification, right-standing with God and the new birth are attained only by faith in the blood of Jesus, Romans 3:21-26. *They are not* attained by keeping the Law because Christ is the end of the Law.

Romans 10:4 Speaks of the Fulfillment of the Law,

> For Christ is the end of the Law [the limit at which it ceases to be, for the Law leads up to Him Who is the fulfillment of its types, and in Him the purpose which it was designed to accomplish is fulfilled. That is, the purpose of the Law is fulfilled in Him] as the means of righteousness (right relationship to God) for everyone who trusts in *and* adheres to *and* relies on Him.

Chapter 3

The Reasons for Marriage

Through revelation of God's Word which is the basis or standard for life, marriage is not merely a civil contract. *The Scriptures state marriage is the most sacred relationship of life and the most powerful union on the face of the earth in the sight of God.* "Moses presents it as the deepest, corporeal and spiritual unity of man and woman in monogamy," Genesis 2:24; Matthew 19:5. [1]

Marriage is for people who have a covenant with Almighty God. Those who choose to believe in and honor the Marriage Covenant will act on what they believe by faith. As a result of their decision to do things *God's Way*, the grace, faith and love of God inside of them will draw the blessings of God for their obedience in this hour and season of time!

There are many reasons blessings and benefits come as a result of being married. Some of them are as follows:

Reason:
Two of the things God gave for our good were (1) the Sabbath to preserve His church (those that receive Him as their Lord and Savior. The assembly of persons who worship Him) and (2) *marriage to preserve mankind.*

Reason:
One of God's basic purposes for marriage is companionship. It is not good for anyone to be too lonely. If marriage is for you and there is good communication in your relationship, this would *offer great companionship.*

Reason:
Without the marital tie, *the family circle,* family institution, parental love and care would have been altogether unknown.

Reason:
When your marriage is a priority and is secure on solid ground, your *children will feel more loved, more secure,* be stronger and have more confidence in themselves.

Reason:
Some believe the number one purpose for marriage is how it represents the mystery of *the gospel in active, living form.*

Reason:
It causes men to be more productive because they have wives to encourage and remind them of certain social obligations. She may influence him to start a business, encourage him to handle responsibilities around the house, or to buy a house if they do not own one. She can suggest to him things they need to do with their children as well as with the extended family and so forth. As a result, the man is more productive in

areas he probably would not think much about if he were single.

Reason:

*In a successful marriage **God's love for us is shown through our love for each other**.* A relationship between a husband and wife is meant to be a living witness to others of the love of Christ Jesus for His church. It is a reflection that our Lord and Savior still loves us in spite of some of the bad decisions we make. As a matter of fact, He gave His life when we, as a people, were being who we are and doing what we wanted. And He gave His life anyway! And offered us eternal life with Him on top of it! WOW!

Reason:
Another great benefit of marriage has to do with the procreation of children. ***Marriage provides fathers and mothers*** as well as protection for children. The Word of God says children are a blessing. Most people are more determined to stay together in order to raise their children.

Reason:
*Marriage will **help regulate sexual behavior** in any society.* Every society needs sexual guide posts or a way to monitor sex so society won't fail and die out like the Roman and Greek societies did. When any society erases their sexual morals, sexual values and allows all types of sexual behavior, it is just a matter of time before judgment on that society will occur, causing it to collapse. Each man having his own wife

helps to keep the society holy (sanctified) and on the up and up doing more good than evil, I Corinthians 7:2.

Reason:
Marriage **protects women by enforcing monogamy.** Society's most serious problem is the unattached male. Women need to be protected from *some* men who are aggressive, self-centered male chauvinists. The danger is women becoming commodities to be used and traded into slavery for sex and other services (which does exist illegally today in many countries). Marriage makes sure there are men and women connected as much as possible to care for and protect one another.

Reason:
When a man and woman marry, procreate children, then nurture and train them up in the way they should go, parents can rest in the fact that when their children are older they will not depart from it, Proverbs 22:6. The result is **with the Word of God as the foundation, you will raise decent and well-adjusted human beings.** Marriage has the potential to produce the next generation of producers, workers, good citizens and good parents with Godly character. With this in mind, marriage plays a significant and important social role in any society. A society has the God-given right to protect children and to have children brought up in nurturing families and homes.

Reason:

A society where marriage is honored is a society that has a lower rate of domestic violence. However, in our world today there is so much pressure on marriage and families which come from outside of their homes. It comes through other natural and spiritual influences and the effects of pressure is shown by the rate of domestic violence and divorces reported each day. One of the major ***reasons for the increase is people are trying to live in a Godly institution without God.***

Reason:

A culture is a system of beliefs, traditions, customs, values, ideas, technology, marketing and so forth. "It constitutes a people's way of life and it is formed because of the needs of the people. The strength of that culture or society is only as strong as the family units who support it." ***Without marriage families are unable to form and create strong societies.*** Marriage calls for love, affection, acceptance, unity, agreement, sharing, total commitment and becoming one. It offers contentment, satisfaction, fulfillment, happiness, joy and companionship.

Years ago, people married because of love and reasons of the heart; wanting to have a family; for security and provision; a desire to share their life with someone; they were not afraid of commitment; many people wanted to be in long term relationships; many simply chose to do things God's way.

Perspectives have changed in many cultures toward the reasons why people marry. Today, many couples want the benefits of a permanent relationship that offers love, security, physical intimacy, happiness and so forth without being committed themselves. Looking for loopholes so they can bail out at any time without any attachments or responsibilities to the household they left. More are asking for pre-nuptial agreements to make sure they do not have to share any of their possessions with someone they said "they wanted to share their life with." Unaware a pre-nuptial only sets things in motion for a separation or divorce when and if you do marry. It sets you up for failure.

One reason being, you are conveying to the other person your possessions are more important than they are. Since you believe one day you will need the pre-nuptial, you are actually calling that day into existence mainly because you believe it. We can have what we say and what we believe.

Couples marry not so much for love but because they were on a mission to "find themselves." Marrying for self-growth and individual satisfaction. People are more into technology than they are people and relationships. These types of marriages are self-centered with selfish motives.

These marriages usually fail. Primarily because they have left God's way for marriage. However, our God is a big God. If we humbly go to Him and ask for forgiveness and repent He is faithful and just to forgive. Then follow His instructions and move forward. (See *God's Way and Divorce Chapters Eleven and Twelve* regarding forgiveness and repentance and additional chapters for ways to prevent divorce.)

Chapter 4

Love is the Essence of Marriage

If *love* is the essence of marriage, then God is the very essence of Marriage, for *God is Love.*

The Bible instructs us to be conscious of the love God has for us at all times. To recognize how He is continuously imparting and sharing His love with us. Understand *God's Love can change and sustain your marriage if you allow it to do so.*

The Word Speaks of God's Love in I John 4:16,

And we know (understand, recognize, are conscious of, by observation and by experience) and believe (adhere to and put faith in and rely on) the love God cherishes for us. **God is love,** and he who dwells *and* continues in love dwells *and* continues in God, and God dwells *and* continues in him. (Emphasis added.)

To love and be loved is one of the greatest and strongest emotions God instilled in mankind at the time of creation. At the same time, He desires that love be returned to Him, *"because He first loved us,"* I John 4:19.

He created people to have someone to love and to also return a portion of that love to Him. So, if we choose to give God His portion *first* then we can love each other with the love of God. He made us in His likeness to enable us to relate to Him and relate to one another with Godly love and character. Love adds meaning and purpose to our lives. When we fall short by making mistakes in life it does not change God's love toward us because His love is not based on us but on Him. Why? *Because He is Love and He does not change,* Hebrews 13:8.

In Romans 5:8 it says, "But God shows *and* clearly proves His [own] love for us by the fact that while we were still sinners, Christ (the Messiah, the Anointed One) died for us." He has proven His love for us is *unconditional love.* We can be assured and rest in knowing God loves us in whatever state we are in.

He knows what is inside of each and every one of us and is willing to stay with us and do all He can to bring us to a place where we achieve the fullness of our purpose. All we need to remember is we are His beloved children and He is our Father, our Friend and our God.

The greatest expression of His love should flow from the creation of marriage throughout the world. Therefore, see the following passages and how they explain *biblically how a husband is to love and respect his wife and how a wife is to respect and love her husband.*

I Peter 3:7 says,

> In the same way you married men should live considerately with [your wives], with an intelligent recognition [of the marriage relation], honoring the woman as [physically] the weaker, but [realizing that you] are joint heirs of the grace (God's unmerited favor) of life, in order that your prayers may not be hindered *and* cut off. [Otherwise you cannot pray effectively.]

Ephesians 5:33 says,

> However, let each man of you [without exception] love his wife as [being in a sense] his very own self; and let the wife see that she respects and reverences her husband [that she notices him, regards him, honors him, prefers him, venerates, and esteems him; and that she defers to him, praises him, and loves and admires him exceedingly]. Also see I Peter 3:2.

Ephesians 5:21-28 tells us,

> Submitting yourselves *one to another* in the fear of God (vs. 21 KJV).

Be *subject to one another* out of reverence for Christ (the Messiah, the Anointed One) vs. 21.

Wives, be subject (be submissive and adapt yourselves) to your own husbands as [a service] to the Lord. For the husband is head of the wife as Christ is the Head of the church, Himself the Savior of [His] body. As the church is subject to Christ, so let wives also be subject in everything to their husbands vs. 22-24.

Husbands love your wives, as Christ loved the church and gave Himself up for her. So that He might sanctify her, having cleansed her by the washing of water with the Word. That He might present the church to Himself in glorious splendor, without spot or wrinkle or any such things [that she might be holy and faultless]. Even so husbands should love their wives as [being in a sense] their own bodies. He who loves his own wife loves himself vs. 25-28. (Emphasis added.)

Men and women are completely equal and can choose to submit (respect and honor) each other. *When we choose to yield or submit ourselves one to another, it means we are choosing to honor and respect the other person as well as to honor God by doing things His way.*

Some of the ways we can show honor to our spouse is by choosing to serve them, to communicate properly and allowing them to fail, realizing they are not perfect, and neither are we. We all need God's grace and mercy and an opportunity to try, even if we make mistakes and fail. People can learn from failures and mistakes.

Women sometimes do more harm than good by trying to prevent their husbands from ever making a mistake. I am not referring to something that will cause major damage or a behavior issue. But when life calls for quick decisions, your husband makes one and you are not in agreement with and it does not work out, show him some grace. Encourage him to pray with you about decisions and when you are both in agreement then venture forth together.

One of the biggest ways you can honor someone is to honor that person where you would like to see them. In other words, treat them as if their destiny has already arrived. Speak life and give favor. Build your spouse up, strengthen them with your words and not tear them down.

Love is a major key to having success in all relationships, especially a marital relationship. When you walk or live a life of love, you are walking with God, *to walk with God is to stay in step with His Holy Spirit*. According to I Peter 1:22, the Holy Spirit is the

One who purifies our hearts so the pure sincere love of God can flow through us and out to others.

"As we allow the love of God to work or flow through us, it will enable us to ever be filled with the Holy Spirit. We are to walk as children of Light and be filled with the Spirit because the fruit of the Light or the Spirit [consists] in every form of kindly goodness, uprightness of heart, and trueness of life," Ephesians 5:8-9, paraphrased.

Some of the things we are *not to do* if we are to be subject to one another: husbands are not to expect their wives to be subservient (so self-abasing as to lack a proper degree of personal dignity). Rather, receive her as a partner to share in mutual biblical submission. Wives *are not to* try to manipulate or reject their husbands to gain control or grounds to force an issue in their favor. All of these childish tactics are not a part of biblical submission. They will only lead to heartache and possibly separation when one or both partners have had enough. *When you decide in your heart to do things man's way and not God's way, you have made a decision for your marriage to fail to be all it could be.*

Paul tried to guard the institution of marriage which God loves dearly. In doing so, Paul gave advice to those who were joined to unbelievers to not disturb their relationship. However, for the good of a marriage, both parties should be in agreement to stay married. Realize marriage is not merely a civil contract when the scriptures make it very clear it is the most sacred relationship in life, I Corinthians 7:13-14.

As you choose love over bitterness, strife or some other demonic spirit, you will have the victory every time. *When love is expressed* through kindness, thoughtfulness, forgiveness, respect, humility, self-control, honor, gentleness, goodness, peace, patience, faithfulness, caring actions and deeds, you are then walking in His love and thereby abiding in Him. This will open the door for God to turn things around. His ways are not our ways, they are higher and will result in a loving and good marriage, Isaiah 55:8-9.

Without love, nothing will be long term in your life because God is Love and apart from Him you can do nothing, John 15:5. God said in His Word without faith we cannot please Him and it is love that activates your faith. You cannot even use your faith to its greatest potential if you are not expressing and receiving the love of God.

God tells us how to love Him with His first and principal commandment (instruction). It is to "love the Lord your God with all your heart and with all your soul and with all your strength and with all your mind; and your neighbor as yourself" Luke 10:27. This is part of our marital covenant with the Lord and as we do our part, He will certainly do His. *He is the only one who can change hearts and all of His commandments can be fulfilled when we keep the Commandant of Love.*

I John 3:23-24 The Message Bible says,

> Again, this is God's command: to believe in his personally named Son, Jesus Christ. He told us to love each other, in line with the original command. As we keep His commands, we live deeply and surely in Him, and He lives in us. And this is how we experience His deep and abiding presence in us: by the Spirit He gave us.

He is a Holy God and He is a Loving God. He set the pace and pattern for marriage and has given us powerful tools and spiritual weapons to maintain it, Ephesians 6:10-18; Luke 10:19. The same holds true for any type of relationship we are in, if we simply choose to model after Him and stay in the love of God, I John 4:10-11.

The Law of Love is found in Luke 6:27-31 and it basically *tells us how to express love to those who have come against us.* For example, verse 27 tells us to make it a practice to love our enemies by doing *good* to those who hate us. One of the first things we are to do is to pray for them. When this is done you open a door for God to heal your heart because of your obedience to a spiritual principle and command. And in Luke 6:31 NAS, the Golden Rule says, "And just as you want people to treat you, treat them in the same way." When we choose to obey God, we free ourselves up from bondage to whatever or whomever.

We can avoid many negative things from coming into our lives if we would just humble ourselves and follow His spiritual instructions. They may not make sense to the natural mind, but if done, it will cause things to turn around for our good. One example of an instruction or command that makes absolutely no sense to the natural mind (I Corinthians 2:14) is to forgive those who have wronged you. Perhaps we have not considered, the Lord has forgiven us of *all our failings and shortcomings* and His desire is we follow His example and do the same toward others, Mark 11:25-26.

If you follow through and do what He has asked, even though it does not make any sense to you, you will find, because of a step of faith, it works. *It will allow you to receive a supernatural healing from a Supernatural God.*

Healing in any area of your life where it is needed is connected to your being able to forgive others. That in turn will close doors that were opened because of unforgiveness which if not dealt with can cause a root of bitterness. When a root of bitterness occurs, every evil practice can be released.

Bitterness opens a door to the enemy then he has access to attack you. You created a place for the adversary to work when you shut God and His ways out. To shut the door on the enemy, repent from your heart, receive forgiveness, speak to God receive new instructions and continue forward.

When we choose to release anger, unforgiveness and bitterness the anointing can flow and our blessings can be unlocked and unblocked. Let God be God! The Bible says "Beloved, never avenge yourselves, but leave the way open for [God's] wrath; for it is written, Vengeance is Mine, I will repay (requite), says the Lord" Romans 12:19.

Therefore, cast your care, stay in a loving frame of mind and move on, I Peter 5:7 and Psalm 55:22 which says, "Cast your burden on the Lord [releasing the weight of it] and He will sustain you; He will never allow the [consistently] righteous to be moved (made to slip, fall, or fail)."

Jesus not only commanded you to not allow your heart to be troubled and afraid, He also said, "[Stop allowing yourselves to be agitated and disturbed; and do not permit yourselves to be fearful and intimidated and cowardly and unsettled]," John 14:27. You have to stop it, you must exercise self-control and other fruit of the Spirit, Gal. 5:22-23.

You have to get hold of yourself and fight off the persistent temptation to give away your peace and keep the gift of rest. In His place of rest, you can commune with Father God and hear instructions and receive His strength through Holy Spirit. Pay attention to the promptings from Holy Spirit.

In continuing our discussion on love, The Song of Solomon illustrates the love between God and Israel, His bride. Just as the book of I Corinthians, Chapter 13 illustrates the love we should have for each other. When we can love the way God says to love, then we will love our Maker and Creator the way He says to love Him, I John 3:23, 24; John 14:15. The Lord says, when you do anything for the least of these in Christ you have done it unto Him, Matthew 25:40.

Guard love and take care of it, because it is the most valuable tool or spiritual weapon you will ever have. There is no weapon formed against love that will *ever* be able to stand.

Great Characteristics of *True or Mature Love* are found in the Love Chapter. I Corinthians 13:4-8, The Book says,

> Love is very patient and kind, never jealous or envious, never boastful or proud, never haughty or selfish or rude. Love does not demand its own way. It is not irritable or touchy. It does not hold grudges and will hardly even notice when others do it wrong. It is never glad about injustice, but rejoices *whenever* truth wins out. If you love someone you will be loyal to him no matter what the cost. You will always believe in him, always expect the best of him, and always stand your ground in defending him.

I Corinthians 13:7-8 the Amplified Bible equally makes a Powerful Statement in Reference to Love,

> Love bears up under anything and everything that comes, is ever ready to believe the best of every person, its hopes are fadeless under all circumstances, and it endures everything [without weakening]. Love never fails...

The Love Chapter describes God's idea of mature love. Notice what is included: patience, kindness, being joyful with truth, trust, loyalty, full of hope and enduring or being totally committed. Unconditional love will allow you to communicate correctly, having the right attitude with your husband, wife, children and others while allowing God to work on any changes needed to be done with all persons involved including yourself.

If your goal or motive is to really show someone else love, then you should remember if it is not *unconditional love* then it really is not love at all. If it is a "heart" issue, only God can change and/or heal a human heart and cause it to align with His will. God will not violate a person's free will nor will He answer any prayers that will violate a person's free will.

So, if you are anxious to see changes in the other person while you are trying very hard to "overlook" all of the faults *you* have determined they have and need to change, know you have a part in helping change to come about.

You are to stand in the gap with your prayers. If you receive instructions from Holy Spirit to confront in a loving way or assist in any way, please be led by your Spirit (heart). The Lord will give you the right words to say and/or what to do if anything at all.

In the meantime, pray only prayers that are in the will of God about the other person. **Never pray soulish prayers.** These are prayers that try to dictate to God what you want to see happen in another person's life that may be against their will or wrong for them. Soulish prayers are controlling prayers which are not of God.

God does not answer these types of prayers because they do not line up with His Will or His Word. *Instead of trying to control someone else through your prayers, pray they will hear God for themselves and listen as He leads them.*

Also, do not allow anyone in your presence to pray controlling prayers over your life. In other words, do not allow someone to use prayer to try and manipulate you into doing what they think you should do. Always go with the peace in your heart and if there is no peace, then you know it is not the will of God for your life.

An unknown author wrote this about love, "Everyone says love hurts, but that is not true. Loneliness hurts. Rejection hurts. Losing someone hurts. Envy hurts. Everyone gets these things confused with love, but in reality, *love is the only thing in this world that covers emotional pain and makes someone feel wonderful again.* Love is the only thing in this world that does not hurt because God is Love!"

Chapter 5

Becoming One with the Right One

It is important to become one in marriage God's Way, the way it was intended to be. In this chapter we will explain the different ways He has given in this area that have been proven to bring success if we choose to do things *His way.*

- We will begin with explaining the spiritual aspect of becoming one with your spouse.

- Further on we will explore how a married couple becomes one in the natural. This is also referred to as "Becoming One Flesh" (your soul: mind, will and emotions).

- Becoming one flesh also involves physical intimacy which will be discussed as well.

- Last but certainly not least, we will discuss how important it is to become one with the "right one," the right person.

Becoming One First in the Spirit and Maintaining Spiritual Growth

In marriage God supernaturally joins couples heart to heart; spirit to spirit at the completion of their wedding vows. As we desire to have a wonderful, meaningful and successful marriage we will need a strong foundation to achieve this. A strategy for marriage will be necessary if we are to achieve this goal.

Therefore, when God, Jesus Christ (The Messiah, The Anointed One) the High Priest of every home, that knows Him as their Lord and Savior, is kept first they in the marriage *will grow closer to Him as individuals, which in turn will draw the married couple closer together.* They will experience a better meaning and understanding for their marriage and of themselves.

The choice to keep God at the center of the relationship will cause one to cleave in a cheerful way. A person will gain greater insight and strategy from a holy God Who loves you and wants to see your marriage succeed. He loves what He created and always desires the best for you. We need to realize the most important thing in our marriage is our relationship with the Most High God.

Marriage is a spiritual bond in a divine institution originally designed to form a permanent union between a man and a woman. With Him we can experience success because our marriage can function properly. This must happen in order to receive all the promises of the marriage covenant which includes a long, loving and healthy marriage.

The first vital thing that should be done is to *cleave to the marriage covenant.* The word *cleave* literally means to "stick like glue." As we cleave to become one this involves coming together on every level: spiritually, physically, emotionally, mentally and socially. As we cleave to our covenant, we should set our priorities to place our marriages at the top of the list, right after our own personal relationship with our Maker.

When we are married we are no longer two, but one flesh, which simply means, of one mind with each other, living together in agreement aligned with the third person in our covenant, and that person is God Himself. He will be the greatest contributor to this marriage as you cleave together to become one. The Bible says, "What therefore God has joined together, let not man put asunder (separate)," Matthew 19:6.

Philippians 2:2 tells us,

> Fill up *and* complete my joy by living in harmony *and* being of the same mind *and* one in purpose, having the same love, being in full accord and of one harmonious mind *and* intention.

Where there is unity, there is blessing and anointing (the power of God). When a couple is thankful for each other and choose to live in harmony and unity they will experience the power of agreement. That will help them make sound decisions which will benefit their marriage and their entire household.

However, if your spouse is not willing to seek God, in order to keep the marriage sound by staying out of danger zones by doing their part, then allow them to see you doing your part. Let them see you walking in love, in forgiveness, being understanding and communicating with good body language, facial expressions and using a calm tone in your voice. Let them see your consideration of them when they know they don't deserve it, as well as allowing them to see you seek God for yourself.

Also let them see you are willing to wait on God for instructions without making any rash decisions about your marriage, which is something God takes very seriously. This can be accomplished by a man or a woman, I Peter 3:1, paraphrased. Of course, I am not speaking about people enduring physical or mental abuse; they will need additional and/or other options.

The New Unger's Bible Dictionary regarding a
Christian marriage and oneness,

> …The original appointment of monogamy is confirmed. The presence of Jesus at the wedding in Cana happily

illustrates the feeling and teaching of Christianity respecting marriage. Christ taught the divine origin and sacredness of this institution. It is more than filial duty. It is unifying. *The husband and wife become one* through the purity and intensity of mutual love; common interests are necessitated by common affection... (Emphasis added.)

The Mutual *Love* is what Makes it *Spiritual* knowing God is *"Love,"* I John 4:16,

...God is love, and he who dwells *and* continues in love dwells *and* continues in God, and God dwells *and* continues in him.

Within the marriage covenant the couple vowed to God certain things. However, as we all know, commandments, teachings or any legalistic "cut and dry" rules and regulations will not prevent people from falling short. *The "hard fast rule" will become destructive when it is without the Spirit of God which gives life and brings balance,* 2 Corinthians 3:6. God does this by His grace, His power which enables you to do what you could not do on your own.

All human beings have basic needs and our spouse is no different. Unfortunately, many spouses go into a marriage expecting their spouse to make them happy, meet their needs and fill the voids in their hearts. For example, the need for acceptance; the need to know who they are. They can only discover or find answers for these types of questions as they learn their true spiritual identity of who they are in Christ.

Also, people have a need for security so as to not be overwhelmed by the world's news and circumstances which is usually very negative. People need to know their purpose. Why are they really here on this earth? Many believe there has to be more to life, a higher purpose if you will, than just punching a clock and making a living or existing just to have a social life and purchase things. And they are right, there is more, much more!

Many marry with the expectations of their spouse filling these and other voids in their lives. When the spouse falls short in doing so their feelings may change and they assume they married the wrong person. But people are not required to keep other people happy, content or fulfilled. Not even a spouse can fill those shoes. *Do not expect from your spouse that which only God can give you.*

A healthy process of coming together in becoming one can be done when the couple is aware of their responsibility in all of this, as well as what is to be expected from their marriage partner.

First of all, each person is responsible for their own personal relationship with God. Which begins with a prayer of salvation if they are not a child of God. They can also rededicate their life to Jesus (Yeshua is His Hebrew name) with a simple prayer if they walked away for a period of time and wish to return to His family and Kingdom for a fresh start. Just ask Him. With that in place they will soon realize through God's Word and teachings that *happiness comes from God meeting their needs and will be the basis for their joy and happiness.*

These types of needs cannot be filled by a husband or a wife but only by a Living God. They will come to understand acceptance from a living and loving God. Who died so their sins could be forgiven and One that says, He will never leave them nor forsake them. He has a plan for their life that is great and fulfilling. He has prosperity for them and at the appropriate time they have a place in heaven. Only He can bring them true comfort (restoration). Knowing they know, that they know, He'll never forsake them.

As far as people needing to know their purpose – God will reveal this when they seek Him. But in the meantime, know all people were created to worship. Some worship their careers, homes, cars, money, a relationship and so forth. Which means they are not worshipping the Living God. When we decide to put Him first and worship Him giving Him that place of honor by following His ways we will mature spiritually, filling the void in our hearts. As we mature He will reveal more about our purpose and help us obtain it.

They will soon understand their true identity is in Christ the Messiah. Therefore, no one else will be able to impact them with anything negative or ugly about themselves because they will know who they are. They also can have a peace about what is happening in the world. The Bible explains the happenings of the times and assures us we are not alone. He makes a way and sends us help and includes angelic assistance.

For example, *when Moses brought the Israelites out of Egypt, it was by God's Grace (Spirit, power and enablement).* At that time, they were all *miraculously healed* after they ate the roasted lamb whose blood was shed and placed over the door and the two side posts of their homes on the night they were delivered out of Egypt, Exodus 12:22.

This is a perfect example of a hidden mystery in the Old Covenant that was revealed in the New Covenant regarding the Christ, the Messiah being the Passover Lamb, Exodus 12:7, 13; Hebrews 10:5; I Corinthians 5:7-8.

He also caused them to have *great favor. So, in addition to being healed,* before they departed they were also made *wealthy* with jewels, silver, gold and clothing from the Egyptians, Exodus 12:35-36. Just one of their benefits of having a covenant with a God Who desires and is willing, powerful and able to give you the best.

God did many miracles for them by His Spirit. They were blessed, empowered, favored and kept by His Grace; not by the laws and regulations. The Lord in Heaven did it all. All they really had to do to continue to benefit under His grace was to follow the leading of His Holy Spirit. Be sensitive to His guidance and instructions. For example, Holy Spirit was present with them in a cloud during the day and a pillar of fire at night to lead them. He had also anointed their leaders to hear Him for instructions and directions.

Even though some were still complaining (which is seen by God as unbelief which is a sin) and in fear, as people are today. *Their wilderness experience was the beginning of trusting Almighty God.* He created them and loved them but had also been silent for four hundred years while they were in captivity. Thus, as a people they had to learn of Him and His ways once again.

One of the major things that had to be learned was it was God's grace keeping them and was in effect before the law was introduced. We understand from that, that **grace is needed to effectively fight and be victorious in spiritual warfare.** There has to be an understanding of the contrast between the Law and the Spirit of Grace and how one should use the written letter of the Word in conjunction with the power of the Spirit of God.

For example, when the Israelites were brought out of Egypt, not only was everyone healed but there were no deaths. When they complained to Moses at the Red Sea, God gave Moses instructions and the Red Sea parted, Exodus 14:19-31. There were no deaths or backlash when they complained about food. *God just gave them what they needed:* water came from a rock, food came from heaven while their clothes and shoes grew as they grew. This is a demonstration of the grace of God.

They experienced miracle after miracle. *Why? Because they were under and protected by His grace.* When the Ten Commandments were introduced, they were meant to instruct as a father would instruct his child for his well-being, Exodus 20. It was also given with the intention people would learn in and of themselves, it was impossible to keep the law with its code of written regulations and *they would need to receive and live by His grace once again.*

In Romans 7:6 NIV it says, "But now, by dying to what once bound us, we have been released from the law so that we serve in the new way of the Spirit, and not in the old way of the written code." Therefore, when the Old Covenant drew to a point, God brought forth a *New Covenant* to *complete or fulfill the old by using a Holy Scripture He first gave* them when He brought them out of bondage.

It was simply, "You must love the Lord your God with all your heart and with all your soul and with all your strength and with all your mind; and your neighbor as yourself," Luke 10:27; Deuteronomy 6:5. In doing so, you will do all God asks of you.

God's Spirit and His Word must flow in your life together in order for you to live the life and have the marriage God intended and purposed for you. If we are doing all that He asks of us, which is to love Him, love each other, as we love ourselves then all of these will entail giving, grace, forgiving and exercising the fruit of the Spirit, Gal. 5:22-23.

As a result, because of His grace, we will choose to honor our father and mother and we will not commit murder, adultery, steal, lie and covet someone else's things, but strive to live a life of liberty and fulfillment in Christ/Messiah.

People will need the grace of God, coupled with a relationship with Him to acquire supernatural help *to keep them in a supernatural covenant. A covenant that has the power to cause two people to become one in the spirit and in the flesh.*

When couples incorporate the Spirit of God Who is already present and a part of their marriage covenant, and they look to Him, the Living God, to help them with their marriage, He is just and faithful to help them maintain and sustain and enjoy their marriage.

Becoming One in the Flesh

Having left your family home with parents (Mt. 19:5) or coming out of the single life, you now bond with your spouse and become one in the sight of God once your vows are spoken. The two of you have supernaturally become one in the spirit, *it is time to learn how to cleave in the natural with your spouse.*

When you and your spouse place the Lord as the head of your marriage by each of you first having a personal relationship with *God*, it will strengthen and preserve your marriage. The Bible says in Ecclesiastes 4:12, "And though a man might prevail against him *who is alone, two will withstand him. A threefold cord is not quickly broken.*"

Becoming One,

If both people in a marriage relationship are born again, then the spiritual union is in place. The most difficult part of the "becoming one" process is usually the uniting of two souls –the joining of two minds, wills, and sets of emotions. Most marital problems in the arena of the soul result from strife over lack of communication, money issues, disciplining Children, sexual misunderstanding, goals. All of these things need to be worked out in the soulish realm of the marriage union, and in order to become one in that area, a husband and a wife need to give their issues to God and say, "Father, change my mind or my will if I'm wrong." God is the One Who will bring them into agreement with His will and purpose. *If each marriage partner is willing to be brought into agreement with the other, they no longer try to force each other to be someone they are not, but realize they need each other to be exactly who God created them to be. They no longer pick on each other's weaknesses. Instead, they partake of their strengths, they enjoy one another, and they enjoy the process of becoming one. By Joyce Meyer, (Emphasis added.)*

Our flesh consists of our body and soul (mind, will and emotions). Therefore, becoming one will involve these four components at given times. For example, our *body* becomes one with our spouse during intimacy. Our *mind* over time becomes like-minded with our spouse. Our *will* begins to be on one accord in agreement with each other about most matters. Which brings us to our emotions. They can be stable, at peace, calm and in balance as we exercise the fruit of the Spirit, Galatians 5:22-23.

As a married couple when we decide to keep God first and align these components with His will, our marriage will "become one" in the flesh God's way! Therefore, this threefold cord of a husband, a wife and God will not quickly or easily be broken.

According to Pastor Ed Young, "What is important to your spouse is important to you. What troubles your spouse, insults your spouse or hurts your spouse, you will feel the weight of these things too." He goes on to say, "We strengthen each other, we encourage each other and we hold each other." In other words, we cleave in both good times and in bad. We are covenant partners.

He added, "When you leave parents, people, problems and places of your past, cleave to the sacred covenant of marriage, to the principles of God and to your mate so you will have unity and are one flesh. If you are to have this oneness in your marriage, he says, *then you must do everything you can to cleave to your mate physically, emotionally, and spiritually.*"

One must be ready emotionally to leave home, realizing that leaving father and mother to cleave to their spouse does not mean you no longer have anything to do with your parents. You should always love, honor, enjoy and respect them. **Leaving your father and mother simply means now your spouse is the exalted person in your life.** You need to reset your priorities to God's order making your spouse the next best person in your life after God.

Married people are the two closest people in the world because *they have spiritually become one* in the sight of God and with that comes added benefits. As already stated, if they pray together in agreement with a prayer that is in God's will, then *their prayer is the most powerful prayer in the universe.* This is one reason Satan fights marriage because prayers that are in agreement come against his kingdom of darkness.

During the cleaving process, in addition to setting your priorities to keep God first, also keep Godly principles and set quality time to spend with your spouse. Touch basis with your spouse during the day and at other times. When thinking about your spouse cleave to the positive things that brought you together in the first place. Think about your spouse's strengths not so much about their weaknesses which we all have.

Let us discuss a few of the needs that can be met by a husband. Women have different needs. Women desire security, knowing they have someone they can share a life with and will do their part so the household runs smoothly. Someone they can trust that is faithful and has integrity. Women would like open and honest communication. Most wives enjoy soft non-sexual affection and attention. Doing things, the two of them really enjoy together.

And women look for their husbands to lead their family. Also, inviting her input to assure sound godly decisions for their household. God has given the right wife (the one God sent) divine wisdom to help in every area of their lives. It is up to him to be humble enough to receive God's gift.

God did send her to be a helpmeet in all areas of their home. She can be a great help to him when he delegates some of his responsibilities to her with full confidence things will be taken care of. God's order is "...the husband is the head of the wife as Christ is the Head of the Church..." and the passage goes on to say, "husbands, love your wives, as Christ loved the church and gave Himself up for her," Ephesians 5:23; 25.

Now let us discuss a few of the needs that can be met by a wife that will continue the process of becoming one. Men generally need honor and respect from their wives. They would like their sexual needs met that are within reason. They would basically enjoy having a friendship with their wife. Having someone they can confide in and not be met with constant negative responses or correction. Someone they feel will keep what they share between the two of them. And of course, domestic help in the home and with their family.

These things can be accomplished through mutual agreement of a wife with her husband on how they could be met. When a wife trusts God He will anoint her to accomplish goals and give her the wisdom and strength needed because He blessed her with a family. God will give the wisdom and help needed to each spouse enabling them to fulfill the role they walk in. Daily communication, decision making, helping and assisting one another with mutual respect and understanding are all working together for the good and will help accomplish the *becoming one* process.

If you are aware of your marriage being orchestrated by the Heavenly Father and confirmed by His Spirit and you are with the right person, yet everything seems to be going wrong, especially in the early stages when you are becoming one, remember this: *His Word* will be *tested and tried.*

If you withstand the test and *flow with* the Holy Spirit and not work against God but with Him, at the appointed time, a turnaround, the deliverance, the help needed, whether it is a change of heart, a new attitude, finances, healing of broken hearts, forgiveness or whatever is needed, will come and it will be "right-on-time." It will refresh you and even deepen your love for one another, enlighten you as a couple, and enhance your relationship creating a bond.

Yes, when the couple remembers they are in a covenant with Christ Jesus, the Messiah, Who is at the head of the relationship that the adversary is trying his best to devour, then they can experience a peace as they seek Him for their help. They can follow His instructions and wait on Him to bring their relationship to what it should be. Strengthen it and prepare it to go to greater levels.

Also keep in mind His instructions may require forgiveness. Seeing a Christian marriage counselor or to stop some destructive habit that is opening doors for demonic oppression may be necessary. As you are *willing* to change things, you can expect the victory.

Becoming One Flesh Also Involves Physical Intimacy

Marriage is the ultimate union on earth. Being one flesh is also expressed through physical intimacy. Sexual intimacy in marriage is a gift from God.

"Sexual Union means oneness and total knowledge of the other person. Sexual intercourse is the most intimate of acts, sealing a social, physical, and spirited relationship. That is why God has reserved it for marriage alone," Life Application Study Bible, Genesis 4:1.

The following revelation and information will give insight into some areas that could assist a couple in a smooth transition regarding sexual intimacy which is important in becoming one and maintaining their marriage.

- *Physical intimacy* will not be all it could be without the proper usage of words; how we communicate with each other during the day. *Words and deeds give a relationship meaning.* What we say and do matters because sex apart from a meaningful relationship will eventually get "old." If the relationship's foundation is only built upon being intimate people eventually move on. *Sexual union is a holy gift from God* to be used within matrimony. When coupled with meaningful, loving words and deeds, this will only add worth and pleasure to the intimacy between a husband and his wife.

- In general, *a well-balanced, healthy intimate relationship* with your spouse could actually pro-long your life span as well as strengthen your marriage. In most cases, your spouse should not need to "wander" or "stray" outside of the home for fulfillment. Small things like holding hands, kissing, hugging and being close to one another are helpful. Working on projects together or doing simple things like watching a movie or walking together will help draw you closer to your mate and encourage intimacy. The fruit of the Spirit such as love, joy, peace, patience, kindness, goodness, faithfulness, gentleness, (meekness, humility), and self-control along with understanding can lead to a healthy fulfilling sexual relationship.

- The purpose of sexual intimacy is more than procreation and pleasure. *It is also to keep us holy, which is why it was created only for those who are married.* Sex engages our bodies and it touches our souls. *A transfer of spirits takes place when people who are not married engage in sex. Soul ties are also formed.* Sexual intimacy is a physical act that is part of a healthy marriage relationship and if it is detached from the relationship, the relationship could become spiritually bankrupt. Sex is a physical act, but it is also spiritual and emotional. It should be guarded and protected by the married couple by not opening a door for any unclean spirits to have place in their marriage.

- When people do not understand the purpose of something they can easily misuse it. Many find out later, after everything has fallen apart, what the true purpose for something or someone truly was. For example, when you are about to use new technology, you read the manual first so you can get the full benefit of the product. However, if you are using it inappropriately or without full knowledge of what it is capable of doing, eventually it will cause some type of breakage or you never discover its full potential. How much more important do you think your sexual life is to God? Follow the manual from the Creator. He knows the purpose of all things, including sex and its importance in the marriage.

- It will take both of you to have a good attitude and the right perspective to meet each other's needs. The way we are designed by God we cannot really meet our own sexual needs. The male and female are different yet we are designed to complement each other. Male and female means it takes two to make one. Sex is something that has to be developed to be pleasing for both. In doing so we discover we need each other. And we discover we fit together by God's design. The more we understand our differences the better we understand one another and are willing to work with the other to achieve the success we are seeking. Both will have to put energy into the relationship regardless of circumstances from within or outside of the home.

- *Coming together is also a form of spiritual warfare* because it will protect most marriages. Being intimate will help prevent you or your spouse from being overpowered with temptation, according to I Corinthians 7:5. The reason I say "most" is because I know of cases where couples were having relations several times a week and one spouse still committed adultery. This happened primarily because there were other major issues in the marriage or with that particular person. However, succumbing to temptation would not be the norm when people are truly committed to God, He is first in their lives, they love one another and are reading the instruction manual (the Bible) for wisdom and direction.

- Another major point is sex does not just happen in the physical realm as mentioned earlier. God intended sex to be spiritual, emotional and physical. Of the three, the spiritual is the most important. Spiritual intimacy involves knowing the whole person and knowing their heart. If you are married and a Believer, studies show

Believers have the best meaningful sexual union. Most Believers understand sex is sacred and given to the married bed by God. Sex is special when you are committed to one another. When you are both committed spiritually it builds a foundation for the marriage as well. As you pray together, worship together, speak about the Word and so on it will strengthen the union and promote transparency and trust.

- When we are emotionally involved it makes a difference as well. For instance, strife can affect intimacy in your marriage. Studies show the top five reasons married couples argue are **(1)** work **(2)** money **(3)** children issues **(4)** sex and **(5)** housework. Also, as part of the emotional aspect of intimacy, we need to validate one another. Listen to each other, comment, compliment, agree or disagree. We need to acknowledge our spouse. Furthermore, agree divorce is not an option. Build a strong foundation for your marriage starting with marrying for the right reasons which does not include selfishness and contracts that protect your interest only. We also need to give our spouse the right to express their opinion without paying a price of the other having a prolonged bad attitude or being cruel in any way. These are only some of the emotional factors which affect the performance of intimacy in a marriage.

- Couples should pray and ask *God to give them wisdom on how to bring balance and pleasure into the intimate part of their marriage.* In being considerate and loving to one another, finding a healthy balance to engage in sexual union that pleases both partners is important. No one should feel as if they are being taken for granted or someone is taking advantage of them. No one should feel as if they are being used just to satisfy the sexual needs of the other, especially when they have needs or desires, in other areas of their marriage that are not being met.

- Keeping balance will assist in preventing one or both from being inconsiderate of violating their spouse's rest. If both of you have *heavy work schedules* (even if mom or dad is a homemaker, there can still be a heavy work schedule), then there need to be solutions to resolve these issues as well. This is key so people do not burn out and want to give up on their entire marriage because one or two areas need to be adjusted or given more consideration.

- *Bringing balance will also help couples to prevent over-taxing each other, by not making unreasonable demands.* This will prevent adding any further stress, of one spouse asking the other to bring into their marriage bed any sexual acts that makes their spouse uncomfortable. This behavior may stem from one spouse having experienced multiple partners before marriage. If their spouse chooses not to participate or bring these acts into their marriage bed this should be respected.

- To resolve the above issues, once again, keeping a balance in your sexual life helps. *A good suggestion would be to plan the best time to be intimate,* whether at night, early morning or whenever. Try having appointed days during the week you are both in agreement with. This will relieve a tremendous amount of stress from overworked individuals. Today stress is basically a part of most cultures because of the pace of living in various societies. One must take charge of their life, finances and happiness because successful things *do not just happen,* they are planned. Having a pleasant union is always intentional.

- This may seem silly to a number of people or couples who think this will interfere with the romantic side of their relationship. But actually, it will enhance it. *With appointed or joint committed times for intimacy,* people can plan ahead to be rested and prepare to make their time together special, joyful, wonderful, creative and a blessing.

- Another area of concern is the *over-taxing of one spouse when the other has a strong sexual drive.* Unfortunately, most couples have been *taught,* even from religion, their spouse's body is given upon request, regardless of the emotional state or if one is exhausted or busy. The teaching, or what has been implied, it is wrong to deny your spouse's request for sexual intimacy *anytime they ask.* Furthermore, *it has been implied that it is a command from God* for them to respond, regardless of circumstances or feelings, because *they are told their body is not their own.* These teachings place emphasis on "since their bodies belong one to another," they cannot refuse, I Corinthians 7:4. *This passage has been misused and misquoted for the marriage bed for perhaps centuries. We hope to add clarity to help people keep a balance and enjoy one another.*

I Corinthians 7: 2-7 says,

> **2-**But because of the temptation to impurity *and* to avoid immorality, let each [man] have his own wife and let each [woman] have her own husband.
>
> **3-**The husband should give to his wife her conjugal rights (goodwill, kindness, and what is due her as his wife), and likewise the wife to her husband.
>
> **4-**For the wife does not have [exclusive] authority *and* control over her own body, but the husband [has his rights]; likewise also the husband does not have [exclusive] authority *and* control over his body, but the wife [has her rights].
>
> **5-**Do not refuse *and* deprive *and* defraud each other [of your due marital rights], except perhaps by mutual consent for a time, so that you may devote yourselves unhindered to prayer. But afterwards resume marital relations, lest Satan tempt you [to sin] through your lack of restraint of sexual desire.
>
> **6-**But I am saying this more as a matter of permission *and* concession, not as a command *or* regulation.

7-I wish that all men were like I myself am [in this matter of self-control]. But each has his own special gift from God, one of this kind and one of another.

As seen in the above passage, verse six (6) clearly states that verses four (4) and five (5) *are not a command from God. Neither are verses four and five a regulation, but a request from Apostle Paul that sexual union is granted by permission and concession.* Conceding means to grant a right or privilege; or to yield. Therefore, *the man or the woman has the right and choice of saying "yes" or "no."*

However, in verse five (5) there is a *warning that if you deprive your spouse of affection for a time without mutual consent* (consent here in the Greek means agreement), *Satan will use the temptations of the culture to become overpowering.* You will run the risk of your spouse being tempted because of a lack of sexual restraint and falling (committing adultery) which will greatly impact your marriage.

Because these scriptures have been misunderstood, quoted out of context or not quoted in its entirety, it has caused guilt, shame and people to be taken advantage of. People, especially women, have been made to feel guilty, as if they were committing a *sin* because on occasions they have told their husbands no to being sexually intimate for one reason or another. Some people have been made to feel ashamed because they have done certain sexual acts that violated their own conscience or upbringing.

Still others are taken advantage of to the point of abuse. How? Some were unknowingly trying to satisfy a *spirit of perversion or lust* that is oppressing their spouse. This means no matter what they did sexually or how many times they yielded, they could not satisfy their mate's desires because their spouse was being driven by a demonic or evil spirit. Some would call it a sex addict. The Bible calls it lust.

Sexual union a gift from God for the married bed. What is stated above is directed to those who seem to be extremely unreasonable with their demand for sexual intercourse from their spouse on a continual constant basis. In most of these cases, they are aware their spouse is not in favor of their advances and they may have voiced it to them. However, the partner who has a strong sexual drive refuses to compromise or listen to reason.

Therefore, only you can discern and determine if there is a problem in this area. Pray and ask God to show you the root of the problem, and what needs to be done to make the adjustments so both parties are in agreement. If you receive instructions then ask God to confirm them for you. If you find this is the case, or maybe it is sexual abuse, professional help from a *Christian Sex Therapist or a deliverance ministry* may be your best solution.

The Strongman Spirit of Perversion is a concern. It has demons attached to it such as: sexual perversion, sexual violence/torture, adultery, pornography, fornication, immorality, incest, seduction, lying and a host of others. *One-way different spirits transfer to people is when they participate in pre-marital sex and form ungodly soul ties with various partners.* Not to mention the risk of contracting a disease.

Unless these married couples get relief from sexual perversion, the spouse that is sexually driven will continue to oppress their spouse for the duration of their marriage. The spirit of perversion could be on assignment to work against the tired spouse with unreasonable sexual demands, who is already tired and overworked from daily responsibilities at their employment and other stresses of the day.

The perverted spirit's assignment is to **wear the person out** so Satan can get a foothold in their life. Satan or master spirits frequently attack or push themselves on people when they are tired. These spirits simply work through people who have an open door where evil forces can use them to wear their spouse out.

One of Satan's many tactics is to wear the Believer in Christ out. He is hoping they will not fulfill their purpose or assignments in life that are from God. The adversary desires that Believers give up and stop moving forward in the Kingdom of God. This is wishful thinking on his part when you know who you are in Christ the Messiah.

Regardless of any evil assignments, faithful people of God will receive the help they need. God will expose evil and give strategies and divine wisdom to those who seek Him. In this type of case healing can always be sought for your spouse through prayer, the Word of God and counseling.

Becoming One with the Right One

When you are with the "right one," together you can build the right foundation for the mission God has commissioned for you both as a married couple. Some of the foundational points are listed above and others are in this section.

Things would be easier if people would *first* pray in faith about the person God has for them. Some may feel this is foolish because after all, they reason, we are grown and quite capable of finding a mate for ourselves. However, statistics coupled with experience, along with speaking to many people over the years from a minister's position, it has been demonstrated choosing a mate in your own strength alone is not always the best option.

One reason being many people hide things and information and even lie about their true motives and themselves. It is also a known fact that people who come into our lives are either sent by God or ordered by Satan. Nothing is by chance! Therefore, there isn't anything wrong with asking God for assistance in this area.

If you are out of the will and timing of God you will more than likely be in places you really do not need to be and meet people that were not in the plan or purpose of God for your life. Satan is constantly trying to pull people out of their cycle of life, their set place, where they will make the right connections for their destiny when they are in God's timing and will.

God will give His children the ability to *discern* by the Spirit of God, I Corinthians 12:10, if someone is not of Him. Their true motives will eventually be exposed. God knows the true heart of an individual and can reveal it. Only He knows the ins and outs of a person as He has stated in His Word. He has even counted the number of hairs on an individual's head.

Until you seek God for revelation about your purpose on this earth you will not have full clarity because only God knows the true purpose for existence. He knows the path that will lead to your destiny. If you are on the right path He knows the plots and devices the enemy will use to try and pull you off your path. Many times, Satan will attempt to pull you out of God's will by sending the wrong people into your life.

Since God created people and marriage, He understands what it will take to "keep it." Why not go to Him first and allow Him to "set it up" and bring it to pass? You can enjoy your marriage because of the marriage covenant and experience longevity in spite of the number of divorces in the world today.

Since He is Omniscient, an all-knowing God, and He knows what we are carrying in way of vision, mission, and destiny that plays a part in His overall plan for His Kingdom and His glory, He will bring two people together. He will cause their assignment to be a success as the vision comes to fruition out of obedience which will give God the glory. They will be blessed for completing their part which in turn will bless others.

If you are a man seeking a wife, the Bible says, *"He who finds a [true] wife finds a good thing and obtains favor from the Lord"* Proverbs 18:22. If you meet someone and feel in your heart, a peace about this person, that this just may be the "one" that God has for you then seek God and ask Him to confirm to you He sent this person into your life. He is just and faithful to do so.

Women are not called to search for a man but to be prepared spiritually, physically and emotionally sound while going about doing good and fulfilling their purpose in life. At the appointed time, the right man will cross your path if marriage is a desire of your heart.

Either gender should never place their life on hold while waiting and watching for the "right person" to come along and enter into their life. They should continue going forward with the desires and goals that are in their heart while they are waiting. Continue to be productive in life and follow the leading of the Holy Spirit. As you take care of God's business God will take care of yours.

As you are being watchful until the right one comes along, *be prayerful for your lifelong partner and marriage even though you may not have met the person as of yet.* Decree your spouse will be the one God has for you and any counterfeits will be exposed and removed from your life.

Pray for your future marriage. Pray you will be equally yoked, have some of the same interests and where there are any differences you are anointed to be the person God called you to be for this marriage and vice versa. Pray the two of you will be thankful and humble and willing to go where God says to go and do what He says to do because you live by faith and trust Him. Your marriage will be protected by the marriage covenant you have with God as well as Holy Spirit and angelic forces will always be there for you as you follow the leading of Holy Spirit.

Pray that you both have divine wisdom, revelation and insight to manage your household; all provision necessary for the family's well-being will be available with God's strategies at work to cause an anointing of multiplication to be in your house. Pray both of you are blessed and have a desire to bless and help others in Jesus' name.

I once heard someone say God wires us to choose a spouse according to His will. It is okay if they're the opposite of you. You will probably still have some similarities, but the differences are also needed so you can be of help to each other where the one is lacking the other will be equipped.

The following is a sample of some of the questions you may have or things to take note of before selecting a mate. Keep in mind people do not have to be perfect; answer everything according to the way you would expect it to be but if, they have a better plan you should support it. Consider some people can and are willing to change. Some people will look you in the face and lie. *The "one thing" you will need to know* as a woman is, did God send this person to be your husband?

The same holds true for a man, did God show you this woman is your wife? Once it has been confirmed you have the person God intended for your life continue to be prayerful. Have the person join you in prayer on occasion, if the person is aware and in agreement. I do not advise telling someone that God told you that he or she is to be your spouse. God can show the person His way and, in His timing, if that is truly the right person.

Marriage Attributes to Consider After Meeting Someone

Compatibility – this would basically be based on their beliefs, values and their Character. Do they have a vision for their life and are they committed to it?

Marital Beliefs – Are they interested in marriage or only living together? Is there longevity of marriages in their extended family? Do they believe in being faithful to one spouse? It will alert you of generational curses that need to be dealt with in prayer.

Their Morals and Values – Do they have integrity? Are they interested in keeping their word? Is this a person you would have as a friend? What are some of their interests and dislikes? Have you already caught them in several lies? Do they respect their own parents? Are they pressuring you into being intimate with them before marriage? How do they propose handling disagreements? Does the person have a violent temper? Do they have several children out of wedlock?

Family – What are their family values? Do they believe family is a priority over friends? Would they like to have children and if so how many? What are their feelings about the family attending church and Bible study. What are their views about extended or blended families? Do they have a relationship with their parents or siblings? What type of discipline would they execute in the home? Do they believe it is alright for a woman to have a career or a business? Do they believe if the woman wants to be a stay-home-mom that is ok? How would decisions in the family be made, would both spouses be heard and they both are in agreement before decisions are made, especially major decisions? If you visit with his family watch how he treats them and others. Is he respectful to older people, children, family and so on?

Faith - Are they of the same faith as you. Christians are not to be unequally yoked with another person in wedlock. Unequally yoked means, if you are a Christian Believer and they choose not to be this would be a major red flag. Because you worship separate gods you cannot fully agree and cleave together as one and be blessed. Christians have supernatural help if they choose to call on God and expect His assistance. They even have the Fruit of the Spirit at their fingertips if they so choose to yield and walk in them, Galatians 5:22-23.

Finances – Discuss their thoughts about how to handle finances including a spending plan. Does the person believe married people should use joint accounts? How do they manage? Are they in heavy debt? Do they tithe or even believe in it? Do they want a pre-nuptial before marriage? Are they selfish or do they have a giving heart? (See *God's Way and Finances* for detail information regarding finances).

Dating or Courtship You Decide

As mentioned earlier prayer is always the first step before entering into dating or courting. Even though dating nor courting are in the Bible, the principal of a man and woman meeting with the intention of marrying is.

One of the purposes of dating or courting is to consider a person's character to help determine if you will be able to spend your life safely with this person. Dating and courting are practiced in our culture today. The objective is to spend time with a person and see if you are compatible and so forth. This is one of the means helpful in determining whether a person is a consideration for marriage. See I Corinthians 7:2; Genesis 24:1-67; and Matthew 19:5-6. Also review chapter one regarding the Origin of Marriage and chapter two regarding the Marriage Protocol for examples of how the marriages came about without a courting period.

"Biblical courtship is a conservative Christian alternative to dating... It is identified by Biblical principles, rather than particular methods or behavioral practices."

The Bible makes it clear fornication is not of God and should not be practiced before marriage. This is an instruction from the Lord for the protection of those who desire to marry and stay healthy spiritually, emotionally and physically. I Corinthians 6:18-20; I Thessalonians 4:1-8.

The purpose of dating or courting is not to fornicate or as it is called today, have "casual sex." There is no such thing as casual sex. That is only a trick and deception from the adversary to cause great heartache when things do not turn out the way they thought it should. Especially according to what happens in the movies and in the media in general. Many base things on what they have seen and heard from entertainers and especially on social media as opposed to truth from the instruction manual, the Word of God (the Bible).

Red Flags May Indicate You are Probably Not with the Right Person for Marriage

If a man is pressuring you for sexual intimacy *before* marriage, more than likely he does not love you. If you think he does then you must be the stronger one and resist his advances. Do not go to places where the temptation will be great for a man. Places where it is very isolated. Avoid agreeing to go to hotels, motels, wild parties and the like. Instead go to the places with or where there are other people.

Use wisdom and watch how you carry yourself in the presence of a man. Do not tease men or lead them on. Be lady like and he should treat you according to how you present yourself. Men are not stupid if you act like a common woman I doubt if he will be asking you for your hand in marriage.

Fornication is a spirit and the Word of God tells us how to handle demonic spirits. James 4:7 says, "So be subject to God. Resist the devil [stand firm against him], and he will flee from you." Whenever using the Word of God speak it forth in faith. Plead the Blood of Jesus over yourself. Rebuke and bind the spirit of fornication. Ask Father God to commission angles to escort you out of any situation that could be dangerous or harmful.

Once you become intimate with a man it opens doors to a lack of trust toward you. It also will cause insecurities in the woman. After all, you just gave what was precious to someone who is probably not going to be committed to you. It also formed soul ties and spirits which can transfer from one to another that are in your bloodline (generations before you). It also opens doors for both of your minds to be tormented with lies about each other through thoughts sent by the adversary. (See *God's Way and Divorce, Chapter Nine* for additional information regarding fornication.)

Always remember your bodies are members of Christ the Messiah and act accordingly, Corinthians 6:15-18. Have respect for yourself and others will show you respect. If you want a blessed and peaceful life then prepare for it by coming in agreement with the Prince of Peace and walk with the King of kings. Just repent where you have fallen short, made mistakes, and ask for forgiveness and continue moving forward. All have fallen short of His glory, Romans 3:23-24. He died to wash away the sin and give you and all of us a new and fresh start each and every day. Let us take His offer as we follow His teachings and example.

Then Expect to Have What He Said You Could Have in Ephesians 3:20,

> Now to Him Who, by (in consequence of) the [action of His] power that is at work within us, is able to [carry out His purpose and] do superabundantly, far over *and* above all that we [dare] ask or think [infinitely beyond our highest prayers, desires, thoughts, hopes, or dreams]--

Is every marriage arranged by God perfect and successful? I would like to answer with a reminder. People are not perfect. Most people come into relationships with past hurts, fears, and some with generational curses they may need to rebuke, bind and cast off. But if God has sent someone into your life then God is in the midst and working behind the scenes for you. The key is to believe God over and above what you see with your natural eyes and trust He will be with you as He said He would. He will give you the strategies and help that you need.

No matter who you are, at times things happen, because we are all human. There are no people without flaws we live in a fallen world. Make a decision you will be willing to assist the person through prayer by drawing close to God, receiving instructions and confirming the instructions. Then putting them into action once the timing is confirmed. Stand in the gap, believe and know God hears you and He will respond.

There is No Comparison with Living in the Spirit as Opposed to Living in the Flesh

Living in the Spirit entails: trusting God, listening and following His instructions, depending on Him for inner strength. Inner strength comes from His marvelous joy, receiving guidance, directions for your life, fellowshipping with like-minded people in the faith, seeing miracles, signs and wonders, moving in the gifts of the spirit, knowing His will through His written Word and so much more!

Living in the flesh entails: doing things in your own strength with your own efforts without any divine intervention. Walking in pride, doubt, fear, anger, being carnal, not having any help from the One Who was sent to be a "Helper" by not being in communication with Holy Spirit.

The same Holy Spirit Who could have been your Vindicator, your Advocate, Deliverer, Healer, Intercessor, Strengthener, Counselor, Standby, Teacher, Comforter, the One who would bring things to your remembrance, the One who saves and enlightens, is the One you will never know as long as you decide to live in a carnal fleshly unsaved lifestyle.

Power can be released from Holy Spirit that will enable a couple's marriage to thrive when they as two separate individuals develop a personal relationship with the King of kings and allow Him to become their Friend. *They will know they can trust Him with one of the greatest gifts He has given to mankind and that is, their marriage.*

Chapter 6

The Marriage Covenant

After God brought the Israelites, whom He married, out of Egypt to be a people unto Himself (Exo. 6:7), He offered a covenant: "I will give you My promises if you will give Me your heart, soul, mind, strength and serve Me with your entire being." Israel agreed.

Exodus 19:4-5 tells us,

> You have seen what I did to the Egyptians, and how I bore you on eagles' wings and brought you to Myself. Now therefore, if you will obey My voice in truth and keep My covenant, then you shall be My own peculiar possession and treasure from among and above all peoples; for *all* the earth is Mine.

Deuteronomy 6:5 tells us,

> And you shall love the Lord your God with all your [mind and] heart and with your entire being and with all your might. (Also see Deuteronomy 11:13.)

The Lord we love has not changed. The New Covenant (of Grace) existed from the beginning. It is key we understand ***God uses a covenant to seal the*** *very foundation of marriage, family and our entire existence with our Maker.*

Without a covenant, marriage is just another arrangement that offers no substance, depth or true value. God gave the marriage covenant to be the anchor which maintains a stable marriage because the covenant is based on their relationship with the Messiah.

The command God gave to the Israelites in the book of Deuteronomy 6:5 and in Deuteronomy 11:13 is the same command He gives in the New Covenant which allows God to extend His grace.

In Matthew 22:37-39 it says,

> ...You shall love the Lord your God with all your heart and with all your soul and with all your mind (intellect). This is the great (most important, principal) and first commandment. And a second is like it: You shall love your neighbor as [you do] yourself. (Also see Luke 10:27.)

It was never meant to be *a relationship* of rules, regulations and laws that drain the very life out of people. The laws or written codes must be balanced with the Spirit of God, otherwise you will have legalism. To fully understand how to love God simply *receive* the Greater Love first, I John 4:7-12.

God always intended for His grace to bring forth the type of relationship He so desired with mankind. Under grace there will always be a balance of the letter of the Word and His Spirit. This is whether we are referring to the "Old Testament" (The Tanakh in Hebrew) or the "New Testament" (B'rit Hadashah in Hebrew) also respectively called the Old Covenant and New Covenant.

God has given a *New Covenant; one of grace* and all those that will receive it will richly benefit from it. For "He has made us competent as ministers of a new covenant – **not of the letter but of the Spirit; for the letter kills, but the Spirit gives life.** Now the Lord is the Spirit, and where the Spirit of the Lord is, there is freedom," 2 Corinthians 3:6, 17 NIV.

Basically, the marriage relationship between God and Israel, as well as a marriage between a man and a woman, rest on a *Covenant.*

Therefore, Let's Explore Covenants, the Different Types and their Meanings:

❖ What is a Covenant?

❖ The Blood Covenant, an Eternal Unbreakable Covenant

❖ The Covenant God Established through Abraham

❖ Will God Ever Break His Covenant with Mankind?

❖ How Does the Covenant Affect Marriages Today?

What is a Covenant?

A covenant is an agreement or a decision to keep a promise. It is made "...either between tribes or nations; or between individuals in which each party binds them self to fulfill certain conditions and was promised certain advantages." [1]

"Why a Covenant is more than a promise. Covenant is a word we use today, but fail to grasp its full meaning. Many think of it as a promise, but a covenant is far more. It is a total commitment, an absolute requirement, to do or not do something, even at the cost of one's life. Commitment, in terms of life or death, is difficult for us to comprehend, but a covenant is exactly that. When cutting, or making a covenant, each party says, 'Everything I have is yours!' That is exactly what we are to do with God." (The One New Man Bible.)

A Covenant Promise - "In making covenants, God was solemnly *invoked as a witness*, hence the expression 'a covenant of the Lord' and an oath was sworn. Therefore, it is improperly used of a covenant between God and man, as man is not in the position of an independent covenanting party. Such a covenant is not strictly a mutual compact but a *promise on the part of God* to arrange His providences for the welfare of those who should render Him obedience" [2] paraphrased.

To further this explanation, it is stated "in the 'covenant,' *man's response contributes to covenant fulfillment*; *yet man's action is not causative* (what brings about the result nor is he the principle or movement to support it). God's grace always goes before and produces man's response." [3]

In other words, even though it is stated "the covenant between God and Abraham" or "God and David" or God and anyone, is to be remembered the outcome is always the result of God's strong hand. Man's part is to love the Lord and follow through with his instructions from God, in obedience to Him.

Furthermore, there are three different types of covenants in the Bible: a covenant is either conditional, unconditional or used to strengthen or support the two previous types of covenants mentioned. A *Conditional Covenant* requires both parties to agree to fulfill a set of conditions in order for the covenant to exist. If either party does not deliver their part then the covenant is broken and invalid.

An *Unconditional Covenant* is only when one party is required to keep the promise and nothing is required of the other party. "The Unconditional Covenant is given by God and is an Eternal Promise not requiring certain behaviors from its beneficiaries. These are identifiable by the use of the verbs *give* and *establish.* When God gives or establishes a covenant, it is unconditional. An exception to this is Lev. 26:1-13, which is conditional. When He cuts a covenant, it is conditional." (The One New Man Bible.)

"The 'Old Testament' and the 'New Testament' as the names for the two sections of the Bible indicate that **God's 'Covenant' is central to the entire Bible.** The Bible relates God's 'covenant' purpose, that a man be joined to Him in loving service and know eternal fellowship with Him through the redemption that is in Jesus Christ." [4]

"The Hebrew word meaning a 'covenant' or agreement (from a verb signifying 'to cut or divide'), is an allusion to a sacrificial custom in connection with 'covenant-making' or where blood flows." [5] "The English word 'covenant' signifies a mutual undertaking between two parties or more, each binding himself to fulfill obligations. It does not in itself contain the idea of joint obligation; it mostly signifies an obligation undertaken by a single person." [6] A covenant can be referred to with different names or terms such as: league, treaty, agreement, promise, vow, pledge and sometimes it is translated as testament.

"Men (mankind) 'enter into' (Deut. 29:12) or 'join' (Jeremiah 50:5) God's covenant..." **God's _covenant_ is a relationship of love and loyalty between the Lord and His chosen people** [7] paraphrased. The people are to cooperate with and observe carefully, the statutes and ordinances of the covenant, Deuteronomy 4:5-8, paraphrased. However, as stated earlier and above all else, God said the greatest command, which is a part of His covenant, is that *His people love Him with their all, their entire being,*[8] Deuteronomy 6:5 paraphrased.

Elaborating on Three of the Many Covenants Found in Scripture

The Shoe Covenant

Is found in Ruth 4:7 (NIV) says, "Now in earlier times in Israel, for the redemption and transfer of property to become final, one party took off his sandal and gave it to the other. This was the method of legalizing transactions in Israel." In the book of Ruth, it also shows a covenant regarding a marriage to a widow of an Israelite involved intricate covenant regulations. It says, "Boaz showed loyalty to God's covenant, respect and love for Ruth and concern for the near kinsman as he worked through the legal process to gain his wife. Such commitment is necessary in marriage," Ruth 3:1--4:12. [9]

The Salt Covenant

Is a covenant which involved people in a loyal act. The salt covenant was a symbol of permanence and preservation. "All of life relates to the commitment we make to God. Certain regulations were part of the covenant along with other provisions. Putting valuable salt on offerings signified costly sacrifice and commitment to God's covenant as well as freedom from impurity" (Leviticus 2:13.)[10] In addition, "covenanting parties were accustomed to partake of salt, thus making a covenant of salt, one that was inviolably sure (Numbers 18:19; 2 Chron. 13:5). The meaning appears to have been that the salt, with its power to strengthen food and keep it from decay, symbolized the unbending truthfulness of that self-surrender to the Lord embodied in the sacrifice, by which all impurity and hypocrisy were repelled." [11]

The Blood Covenant, an Eternal Unbreakable Covenant

Mankind was redeemed by the price of blood. The New Covenant in Christ differs from the Old Covenant because it is eternal. *The Lamb of God, the Lord Jesus, shed His blood to seal this covenant forever making it the strongest covenant in the earth today.* Because of His sacrifice this covenant also blesses us with every spiritual blessing in the heavenly realm, Ephesians 1:3.

Hebrews 13:20-21 says,

> Now may the God of peace [Who is the Author and the Giver of peace], Who brought again from among the dead our Lord Jesus, that great Shepherd of the sheep, by the blood [that sealed, ratified]

the everlasting agreement (covenant, testament), strengthen (complete, perfect) and make you what you ought to be and equip you with everything good that you may carry out His will; [while He Himself] works in you and accomplishes that which is pleasing in His sight, through Jesus Christ (the Messiah); to Whom be the glory forever the ages of the ages) Amen (so be it).

2 Chronicles 13:5 says,

Ought you not to know that the Lord, the God of Israel, gave the kingship over Israel to David forever, even to him and to his sons by a covenant of salt?

Why is the blood of Jesus so important? Because it was foretold in the Holy Scriptures a virgin would give birth to the Son of God (Isaiah 7:14; Luke 1:26-35 and Matthew 1:18-25) and He would be sent not to condemn the world, but rather the world through Him might be saved (find salvation and be made safe and sound through Him, John 3:16-17). *And because He was the Son of God His blood was WITHOUT the Adamic stain of sin.*

Furthermore, He shared in the humanity of His children having flesh and blood and through His death He broke the power of him who held them by the power of death.

Hebrews 2:14-15 says,

> Since, therefore, [these His] children share in flesh and blood [in the physical nature of human beings], He [Himself] in a similar manner partook of the same [nature], that by [going through] death He might bring to nought *and* make of no effect him who had the power of death - - that is, the devil – And also that He might deliver *and* completely set free all those who through the [haunting] fear of death were held in bondage throughout the whole course of their lives.

The Heavenly Father prepared Him a body that would have blood that was <u>not</u> *corrupted by the curse* which was released on mankind after the first Adam disobeyed God, Heb. 10:5-10; Genesis 3. So, when this blood was sacrificed through the obedience of Jesus, the Heavenly Father received it and reconciled mankind back to Himself, Romans 5:19.

Hebrews 10:5-10 Explains the Reason *God Prepared a Body* for Jesus,

> Hence, when He [Christ] entered into the world, He said, Sacrifices and offerings You have not desired, but instead *You have made ready a body for Me [to offer];*

In burnt offerings and sin offerings You have taken no delight. Then I said, Behold, here I am, coming to do Your will, O God – [to fulfill] what is written of Me in the volume of the Book...Thus He does away with and annuls the first (former) order [as a means of expiating sin] so that He might inaugurate and establish the second (latter) order.

And in accordance with this will [of God], we have been made holy (consecrated and sanctified) through the offering made *once* for all of the body of Jesus Christ (the Anointed One). (Emphasis added.)

In the book, *The Power of the Blood,* the author further explains how **God the Father Prepared a Body for His Son with Perfect Blood,** [12]

His blood was perfect and the Holy Spirit was the Divine Agent who caused Jesus' conception in Mary's womb. This, therefore, was **not a normal conception, but a supernatural act of God in planting the life of his already existent Son right in the womb of Mary,** *with no* normal conception of a male spermatozoon with the female ovum of

Mary. As the blood type of the Son of God was a separate and precious type, it is inconceivable that Mary could have supplied any of her Adamic blood for the spotless Lamb of God. All the Child's Blood came from His Father in heaven by a supernatural creative act of God. **Jesus' Blood was without the Adamic stain of sin.**

The idea by a few that Mary supplied the ovum and that the Holy Spirit supplied the spiritual spermatozoon would mean that Jesus would have been conceived with mixed blood, part of Adam and part of God, which is repugnant to God's plan of salvation for a fallen human race.

The fact of the matter is that God says in the Bible that He prepared a body for His Son. It was that body that was created in Mary's (Miriam in Hebrew) womb, (Emphasis added.)

Jesus' Conception was Not Normal but Supernatural. The Following is a Normal Conception, [13]

The female ovum itself has no blood, neither has the male spermatozoon; but it is when these come together in the fallopian tube that conception takes place, and a new life begins. The blood cells in this new creation are from both father and mother and the blood type is determined at the moment of conception and is thereafter protected by the placenta from any flow of the mother's blood into the fetus.

The Reason His Blood had to be Perfect and not Mixed with the First Adam (Paraphrased), [14]

Of course the obvious is that *Jesus' blood could not be tainted with the cursed blood if He was to accomplish His mission and He did.* Therefore, when God created man, He formed a body from the dust of the ground (Gen. 3:19) – from the substances and chemicals of this planet. *Then He breathed into this body the breath of life.* In other words, He breathed into this chemical composition some of His own spiritual life, and that life was held in the chemical substance we call blood.

So, you see, blood is not life, but it carries life. This becomes quite clear by observing what happens at death. Immediately after expiration, the person is still warm, and will remain so for a brief time. Yet that person is dead because the mysterious *life* has departed from the blood. The life of man is carried in his blood stream. *Life itself is spiritual, but it must have a physical carrier, and this carrier is the blood.* Our blood has the capacity to carry the life of God, the contact between the Divine and the human rests in the blood stream.

Jesus was the only begotten of the Father (John 1:14) and His body was formed and fashioned wonderfully in the womb of Mary His mother; but **the Life that was in Jesus Christ came alone from the Father by the Holy Spirit.** No wonder He said I am the LIFE (John 14:6), emphasis added.

When disobedience corrupted the life in our blood, it was no longer pure breath of life from God and it was causing us to die. However, because of God's mercy, *His desire for a family*, fellowship and His love for us all, He sent His only begotten Son. The result is we can overcome evil by the blood of the Lamb, Revelation 12:11.

To further explain the meaning of a covenant, one must understand *there were ceremonies involved to seal them.* However, they had to be repeated regularly and for man's sins, repeated yearly, until the blood covenant put a stop to it forever. This will be explained after a quick definition of what a ceremony would entail.

"Covenants were not only concluded with an oath (Gen. 26:28; 31:53; Josh. 9:15), but after an ancient custom, confirmed by slaughtering and cutting a victim into half between which the parties passed, to intimate that if either of them broke the covenant it would fare with him as with the slain and divided beast. Moreover, the covenanting parties often partook of a common meal (Gen. 26:30; 31:54) or at least of some grains of salt." [15]

> "According to the Mosaic ritual, the blood of the victim was divided into halves; one-half was sprinkled upon the altar and the other upon the people (Ex. 24:6-8).
>
> The meaning of this seems to be that, in the sprinkling of the blood upon the altar, the people were introduced into gracious fellowship with God, and atonement made for their sin. Through the sprinkling of the blood upon the people Israel was formally consecrated to the position of God's covenant people." [16]

The Covenant God Established Through Abraham

In Genesis 6:18-20 God established and ratified a covenant with Noah before the flood occurred that lasted for forty days and forty nights. The next covenant God established with mankind was with a *Hebrew named Abram* in Genesis 15:5, 9-21. However, before the covenant was established Abram was called by God and the Lord spoke to him.

Genesis 12:1-3,

Now [in Haran] the Lord said to Abram, Go for yourself [for your own advantage] away from your country, from your relatives and your father's house, to the land that I will show you. [Hebrews 11:8-10].

And I will make of you a *great nation*, and I will bless you [with *abundant increase* of favors] and make your *name famous* and distinguished, and *you will be a blessing* [dispensing good to others].

And I will bless those who bless you who confer prosperity or happiness upon you] and curse him who curses or uses insolent language toward you; in you will families and kindred of the earth be blessed [and by you they will bless themselves]. [Gal. 3:8]. (Emphasis added.)

God also told him to "look now toward the heavens and count the stars--if you are able to number them." Then He said to him, "So shall your descendants be." In other words, he would have so many descendants he could not count them, Gen. 15:5 and Hebrews 11:12.

Fourteen years later, God renewed the covenant with Abram and changed his name from Abram, which means *exalted father*, to Abraham, which means *father of many*. He also established circumcision as a part of the covenant, Genesis 17:4-21.

God made a promise to Abraham that is still in effect to this day. This covenant is unconditional because God will never fail to do His required part of keeping His promise, therefore, the Abrahamic covenant will never be broken. The main features of the Abrahamic covenant were basically for a nation and a land: (1) The promise of the descendants; (2) the promise of the land; and (3) the promise of blessing and redemption.

One of the key principles of the Abrahamic covenant is when a person or a nation obeys God concerning the moral truths found in the Holy Bible, that person or nation would be blessed. To be blessed means to be increased.

When God gave Abraham a covenant, it was a *covenant of grace and faith.* Abraham also increased greatly as God made him extremely rich in livestock, in silver and in gold (Genesis 13:2). God also gave land to his posterity (succeeding generations), Genesis 12:7.

Genesis 17:7 tells us,

> And I will establish My covenant between Me and you and your descendants after you throughout their generations for an everlasting, solemn pledge, to be a God to you and to your posterity after you.

This passage shows God not only made a covenant with Abraham but also with Abraham's descendants through his marriage to Sarai whose name was also changed as quoted below.

Genesis 17:15-21 tells us,

> And God said to Abraham, As for Sarai your wife, you shall not call her name Sarai, but Sarah [Princess] her name shall be. **And *I will bless her and give you a son also by her.*** Yes, I will bless her, and she shall be a mother of nations; kings of peoples shall come from her.
>
> Then Abraham fell on his face and laughed and said in his heart, Shall a child be born to a man who is a hundred

years old? And shall Sarah, who is ninety years old, bear a son? And [he] said to God, Oh, that Ishmael might live before You!

But God said, Sarah your wife shall bear you a son indeed, and you shall *call his name Isaac* [laughter]; and I will *establish My covenant* or solemn pledge *with him for an everlasting covenant and with his posterity after him.*

But My covenant, My promise and pledge, I will establish with Isaac, *whom Sarah will bear to you at this season next year.* (Emphasis added.)

Taking this a step further, the Lord made it clear the covenant would be throughout generations, for an everlasting, solemn pledge. This brings us in remembrance that *this covenant will not be broken because it is sealed with the blood of Jesus (Yeshua) Who is the Heir of the covenant made between God and Abraham.*

Galatians 3:16-29 tells us,

Now the promises (covenants, agreements) were decreed and made to Abraham and his Seed (his Offspring, his Heir). He [God] does not say, And to seeds (descendants, heirs), as if referring to many persons, but And to your Seed (your Descendant, your Heir), obviously referring to one individual, Who is [none other than] Christ (the Messiah) ...For if the inheritance [of the promise depends on observing] the Law [as these false teachers would like you to believe], it no longer [depends] on the promise; however, God gave it to Abraham [as a free gift solely] by virtue of His promise. What then was the purpose of the Law? It was added [later on, after the promise, to disclose and expose to men their guilt] because of transgressions *and* [to make men more conscious of the sinfulness] of sin; and it was intended to be in effect until the Seed (the Descendant, the Heir) should come, to *and* concerning Whom the promise had been made...

Is the Law then contrary *and* opposed to the promises of God? Of course not! For if a Law had been given which could confer [spiritual] life, then righteousness *and* right standing with God would certainly have come by Law... But the Scriptures [picture all mankind as sinners] shut up *and* imprisoned by sin, so that [the inheritance, blessing] which was through faith in Jesus Christ (the

Messiah) might be given (released, delivered, and committed) to [all] those who believe [who adhere to and trust in and rely on Him] ... So that the Law served [to us Jews] as our trainer [our guardian, our guide to Christ, to lead us] until Christ [came], that we might be justified (declared righteous, put in right standing with God) by *and* through faith... And if you belong to Christ [are in Him Who is Abraham's Seed], then you are Abraham's offspring and [spiritual] heirs according to promise.

Galatians 3:16-29 above states the Heir is Jesus and all connected to Him are part of the succeeding generations. I listed this passage to prove *when you are a descendant of Abraham, you are entitled to receive the Blessings of Abraham* because of the covenant that was made between God and Abraham.

This blessing will be greatly appreciated when you are standing on and believing from the Word of God to receive your inheritance. This will include your marriage and family having the peace and prosperity God chose for you to have as heirs of the covenant of Abraham.

God is mindful of us and will bless us, the Word says, "May the Lord give you increase more and more, you and your children," Psalms 115:12-16. Material blessings were a part of the covenant of increase for

Abraham and his descendants to enjoy while they were here on this earth. The *Blessing of Abraham* also includes the blessings that were received for obedience found in Deuteronomy 28:1-14.

All of these material blessings were enjoyed by Abraham and his children because *they never allowed the blessings to become their god. God was first* in Abraham's life, not the material riches, therefore God did not mind him and his family enjoying the blessings on this earth that brought comfort into their lives. The same holds true for all succeeding generations in Christ.

Galatians 3:26-29 References Abraham's Seed,

> For in Christ Jesus you are all sons of God through faith. For as many [of you] as were baptized into Christ [into a spiritual union and communion with Christ, the Anointed One, the Messiah] have put on (clothed yourselves with) Christ. There is [now no distinction] neither Jew nor Greek, there is neither slave nor free, there is not male and female; for you are all one in Christ Jesus. And if you belong to Christ [are in Him Who is Abraham's Seed], then you are Abraham's offspring and [spiritual] heirs according to promise.

The Lord reminds us not to be a stranger to our covenant and promises because we receive our hope from the covenant God made with Abraham. The covenant reminds us we are not alone without hope or without God in this world but are close because of the blood of Jesus, Ephesians 2:12-14.

History about one's self, whether it is spiritual or in the natural, is always helpful in receiving one's destiny and preventing it from being stolen. When you can walk or live with confidence knowing your rights, in this case rights of an inheritance because of who you are in Christ. It makes one aware there is more to life than they could have ever imagined. It also gives life more meaning and understanding.

To think God in Heaven made a *covenant with your forefather* (if you are a descendant of Abraham) *that still stands and is active today.* That covenant is eternal and carries with it tangible blessings to make your life enjoyable on earth as the process of His restoring families takes place.

Lastly, God gave a *sign with each covenant.* A sign is *evidence of God's promises.* He has done something in the realm of the physical to let us know He is present and involved, 2 Corinthians 1:20. Examples of signs are given below and follow throughout the chapter. For example, one of the signs of accepting and ratifying the covenant God made with Abraham was the circumcision of all males, (Genesis 17:11-13). This is still in effect today, however *circumcision is no longer used to show or prove a covenant exists today for all those in Christ* Messiah.

Colossians 2:11 tells us,

> In Him also you were circumcised with a circumcision not made with hands, but in a [spiritual] circumcision [performed by] Christ by stripping off the body of the flesh (the whole corrupt, carnal nature with its passions and lusts).

Another example, God established a covenant with Noah, with his descendants and with every living creature with him: the birds, the livestock and all the wild animals, all those that came out of the ark with him. He said "never again will all life be cut off by the waters of a flood; never again will there be a flood to destroy the earth," Genesis 9:9-11 NIV.

God said He set a rainbow in the clouds and it will be a sign of the everlasting covenant between Him and the earth, Genesis 9:11-16. ***Rainbows still exist today which indicates the covenant still stands today.***

In addition to God giving signs to His people to show evidence of His promises, He will also give signs to show them the correct way to go. Once the Lord sent us on a journey to Bel Air, California and said look for the red sign. We were actually looking for a "sign" and it turned out to be a red vehicle my husband recognized which led us to the right house and in turn making the right connection for our next home.

During wilderness experiences on the way to our promise land, destiny or to fulfill a dream God places in our hearts, we will receive confirmation and sometimes a sign on our journey. Confirmation and/or signs to encourage, confirm and help keep us on track and in God's timing.

God does not consider signs wicked, but He gives direction through them because of His love and mercy. What *displeases* Him are people who *demand* a sign to prove He is who He claims to be, Matthew 12:38-39. Everyone is born with enough faith to believe the Messiah came, died and rose from the grave. Those who demand a sign to prove Who He is need to exercise their faith and simply take Him at His Word. In doing so, they will please the Living God, Who out of His mercy and kindness extends His grace and at times will give a sign to make our journey a more pleasant and accurate one.

Will God Ever Break His Covenant with Mankind?

His Word says, "For the Lord your God is a merciful God; He will not fail you or destroy you or forget the covenant of your fathers, which He swore to them," Deuteronomy 4:31. Under the Old Covenant God was *with us* and under the New Covenant God is *in us*.

In Leviticus 26:42-45 the Lord said,

> Then will I [earnestly] remember My covenant with Jacob, My covenant with Isaac, and My covenant with Abraham and [earnestly] remember the land... v 45 says, But I will for their sake [earnestly] remember the covenant with their forefathers whom I brought forth out of the land of Egypt in the sight of the nations, that I might be their God. I am the Lord.

God takes His covenants very seriously. "To make a promise to God and not carry through represents lack of gratitude or trust in God. We must not make promises to God lightly. He does not take His words or ours lightly. He expects us to do what we promise, no turning back" paraphrased, (Ecclesiastes 5:4-6 NIV). [17] In His Word He tells us, "When you vow a vow *or* make a pledge to God, do not put off paying it; for God has no pleasure in fools (those who witlessly mock Him). Pay what you vow. It is better that you should not vow than that you should vow and not pay," Ecclesiastes 5:4-5.

Therefore, a man *can* break his covenant with God as it will be demonstrated in this chapter. However, let's look at what God said He would do with His covenant between Himself and His people that would cause it to last forever.

Jeremiah 31:31-34 states,

Behold, the days are coming, says the Lord, when I will make a new covenant with the house of Israel and with the house of Judah. Not according to the covenant which I made with their fathers in the day when I took them by the hand to bring them out of the land of Egypt, My covenant which they broke, although I was their Husband, says the Lord. *But this is the covenant which I will make with the house of Israel: After those days, says the Lord, I will put My law within them, and on their hearts will I write it; and I will be their God, and they will be My people.* And they will no more teach each man his neighbor and each man his brother, saying, Know the Lord, for they will all know Me [recognize, understand, and be acquainted with Me], from the least of them to the greatest, says the Lord. For I will forgive their iniquity, and I will [seriously] remember their sin no more. (Emphasis added.)

Because of the New Covenant which God said He would make with the house of Israel and with the house of Judah, anything man does to jeopardize or break the covenant between God and mankind can quickly be restored by asking for forgiveness and with true repentance.

Furthermore, in the book of Jeremiah 33:20-26, the Lord explains you cannot break His covenant with the day or His covenant with the night. Just as that will be forever so shall it be a sign the covenant He made with David and the covenant He made with the Levitical priests and His ministers cannot be broken either and will be forever.

God announced a New Covenant in the Old Testament and the *New Testament* confirms and establishes it. We find the words were written in the book of Jeremiah 31:31-34, were also listed in the book of Hebrews 8:8-12, as a reminder and to reinforce the covenant. In the book of Hebrews 8:8, it says to whom the covenant is directed to "...I will make and ratify a new covenant or agreement with the house of Israel and with the house of Judah."

In the book of Hebrews 10:16-18, the Lord makes the agreement plain: "This is the agreement (testament, covenant) that I will set up and conclude with them after those days, says the Lord: I will imprint My laws upon their hearts, and I will inscribe them on their minds (on their inmost thoughts and understanding), ...and their sins and their lawbreaking I will remember no more. Now where there is absolute remission (forgiveness and cancellation of the penalty) of these [sins and lawbreaking], there is no longer any offering made to atone for sin."

Why is there no longer any yearly offering made to atone for sin? *Because there is now "full freedom and confidence to enter into the [Holy of] Holies [by the power and virtue] in the blood of Jesus," Hebrews 10:19; 9:11-28.* The door was opened on the day of Calvary when the veil was torn from top to bottom by God Himself after the price was paid to redeem man and reconcile him back to God and re-establish fellowship with Him. Because of the sacrifice, the covenant was restored and made new and we are welcomed to be a part of it because of His grace to receive all by faith (to simply trust and take Him at His Word), Ephesians 2:5 and John 3:14-17.

The Book of Isaiah 9:6-7 Confirms God Set a New Covenant in Place that *Will Not Be Broken* by Him,

For to us a Child is born, to us a Son is given; and the government shall be upon His shoulder, and His name shall be called Wonderful Counselor, Mighty God, Everlasting Father [of Eternity], Prince of Peace. Of the increase of His government and of peace there shall be no end, upon the *throne of David* and over his kingdom, to establish it and to uphold it with justice and with righteousness from the [latter] time forth, even *forevermore*. The zeal of the Lord of hosts will perform this. (Daniel 2:44;

Hebrews 1:8 and I Corinthians 15:25-28). (Emphasis added.)

"That hope looked for a future king who would bring about the reign of God and the redemption of His people. This passage describes the hope -- for the messianic ruler to reign on the *throne of David.* His kingdom would be established on the basis of justice and righteousness. It would be a lasting kingdom, taking the Lord Almighty Himself to accomplish it. The *New Testament (Covenant)* recognized Jesus as the fulfillment of this hope, the Inaugurator of God's ideal reign, who will return to consummate it." [18]

Further, *"the Covenant with David was in reality but another and more specific form of the covenant with Abraham*; its main object was to mark with greater exactness the line through which "The Blessing" promised in the Abrahamic covenant was to find it's accomplishment. The royal *Seed* was from then on to be in the house of David (2 Samuel 7:12; 22:51), and especially in connection with the *One* who was to be preeminently the Child of promise in that house, all good, *first* to Israel and then to all nations, should be realized," Psalms 2:22; Isaiah 9:6-7.[19]

Also, in the book of Matthew 1:1-16 in the genealogy of Jesus with emphasis on verse sixteen, this passage also clearly gives the connection where it proves *Jesus came through the line of King David who was from the line of Abraham.* Abraham's covenant was for a nation and a land whereas David's covenant was for a throne and a city, Jerusalem. It was all constructed to enable the Child of promise to come forth and rule forever.

The Lord always, as mentioned earlier, gives a *sign to confirm or show evidence He has made a covenant.* The following scripture shows God gave a *sign* that demonstrates He established a New Covenant with King David that would last forever.

Psalms 89:34-37 tells us,

> My covenant will I not break or profane, nor alter the thing that is gone out of My lips. Once [for all] have I sworn by My holiness, which cannot be violated; I will not lie to David: His Offspring shall endure forever, and his throne [shall continue] as the sun before Me. [Isa. 9:7; Gal. 3:16]. It shall be established forever as the moon, the faithful witness in the heavens. [Rev. 1:5, 3:14].

The *New Covenant was also sealed* and is why it was received by our Father in Heaven as the final sacrifice to redeem mankind.

In Hebrews 9:11-28, I have Listed verses 11, 12 and 15 to Demonstrate this Point,

> But [that appointed time came] when Christ (the Messiah) appeared as a High

Priest of the better things that have come and are to come. [Then] through the greater and more perfect tabernacle not made with [human] hands, that is not a part of this material creation. v12 - He went once for all into the [Holy of] Holies [of Heaven], not by virtue of the blood of goats and calves [by which to make reconciliation between God and man], but His own blood, having found and secured a complete redemption (an everlasting release for us). v15 – [Christ, the Messiah] is therefore the Negotiator and Mediator of an [entirely] new agreement (testament, covenant), so that those who are called and offered it may receive the fulfillment of the promised everlasting inheritance –since a death has taken place which rescues and delivers and redeems them from the transgressions committed under the [old] first agreement.

God is not a man that He should lie. He is faithful to His Word. If He said it, He will do it. This is why we place our trust in Him and in His Word. 2 Timothy 2:13 in the Message Bible it says in regards to His faithfulness, "If we give up on him, he does not give up -- for there's no way he can be false to himself."

Furthermore, *God is faithful from the beginning to the end.* He demonstrates His faithfulness as He calls us to salvation and as He calls us to be sanctified. He knows we cannot achieve these things in our own power and wisdom, so He graces us with His grace (ability and empowerment) and gives us His wisdom to show His faithfulness and in order to fulfill His promises to us. Therefore, we have no need to fear the judgment which the world (people who are without salvation in Christ Jesus) will face at the appointed time.

I Thessalonians 5:24 tells us,

> Faithful is He Who is calling you [to Himself] and utterly trustworthy, and He will also do it [fulfill His call by hallowing and keeping you].

In concluding this portion and answering the question of will God break His covenant with mankind, the fact was established He will not. However, *as mentioned earlier, mankind, on the other hand, could break his covenant with the living God. King Solomon was able to break the covenant* God had with him, but because of God's *faithfulness* to His Word, God had *already protected* the covenant by making a new covenant with Solomon's father King David. The fact King Solomon had nullified his covenant with God is explained in the following passage:

Parallel Version Footnote, I Chronicles 28:9 KJV/AMP states,

> God's promises to men and women invariably are dependent upon the other party to the covenant meeting His conditions, whether He says so at the time or not. In I Chronicles 28:7 we find Him promising to establish Solomon's Kingdom forever. Yet *in I Kings 11:9-11 we find that God became angry with Solomon for all his degenerate and abominable conduct and his treachery of heart toward Him; and without mercy, except for David's sake, God declared that the kingdom would be torn from him.*
>
> *Was God breaking His covenant with Solomon? No. Solomon had broken and nullified that covenant long before; it no longer existed. There was now no promise for God to keep.*

Some Christians are prone to think that God will keep His part of a bargain whether they do or not, but the wisest man who ever lived died knowing that God is not mocked. "[He inevitably deludes himself who attempts to delude God.] For whatever a man sows, that only is what he will reap" (Galatians

6:7). "If you seek Him [inquiring for and of Him and requiring Him as your first and vital necessity], you will find Him; but if you forsake Him, He will cast you off forever! (Author's addition -- "But whoever denies and disowns Me before men, I will also deny and disown him before My Father Who is in heaven," Matthew 10:33).

Unfortunately, in all of Solomon's wisdom, he failed to comprehend that "Something greater and more exalted and more majestic than the temple is here!" And Someone more and greater than Solomon is here (Matthew 12:6, 42).

People of God please realize when the God of the third heaven created us by His power and grace in His own image, He gave everyone a free will. He will not violate that. He will not make us love Him, obey Him or do anything else. He will lead us into all righteousness through Christ Jesus by His Holy Spirit who was sent to help keep us on track.

However, if we choose to ignore His Holy Spirit and His plan for our lives (which is greater than any we could ever possibly come up with ourselves), then He has no choice. Because of our free will, He will allow us to proceed in whatever we decide to do which can and will be influenced by the adversary.

These are a few of the reasons God takes His covenants very seriously. His Word is His bond. They are living words; containers of power that are not to be taken lightly. He will remain faithful to His Word even when we are not.

How Does the Covenant Affect Marriages Today?

We have shown the new covenant God made was through the line of David and it will last forever. This is important because the essential core for the entire marriage covenant between a man and a woman is modeled after the marriage of God and Israel. *Therefore, since that covenant still stands, so does the covenant God will validate for today's marriages.*

Remembering two things: First, the new covenant made through the line of David not only includes the covenant made with our forefathers, Abraham, Isaac and Jacob, but the *land of Israel* is also mentioned. It's mentioned in the new covenant in several passages as a reminder God does not forget His promises. Second, Jesus showed all of us throughout time the importance of the wedding and marriage covenant when He did *His very first miracle* at a wedding feast, John 2:1-11.

Marriage is a Divine Institution which is Validated Only by God Simply Because He Created It

Short Summary: He is the only One qualified to do so. It is between one man and one woman and God. At the time God was restoring the earth, the Lord God formed mankind (male and female) from the dust of the ground and breathed into his nostrils the Spirit of life, Genesis 2:7; Gen.1:27. He created mankind in His own image, or likeness, and gave *them complete authority* over all the earth, Genesis 1:26.

Shortly after God formed man, He brought forth his wife who was hidden inside of him. God said it was not good (sufficient, satisfactory) that the man should be alone... Genesis 2:18.

Therefore, "the Lord God caused a deep sleep to fall upon Adam; and while he slept, He took one of his ribs or a part of his side and closed up the [places with] flesh" Genesis 2:21.

However, when God opened and closed Adam's side **blood was shed.** "And the rib or part of his side which the Lord God had taken from the man *He built up and made into a woman, and He brought her to the man,"* Genesis 2:22.

When God *brought* her to the man the first marriage between one man and one woman was ordained. Furthermore, in doing so, **the Lord of Glory, validated the first Blood Covenant made on earth between God and mankind.**

Furthermore, in a biblical wedding ceremony, the woman is usually escorted by her father down the aisle and is presented or *brought* to her husband. Here again is another model that was adapted by man from God's protocol of His marriage to Israel, for God said "He *brought* Israel to Himself," Exodus 19:4.

Now many believe on the wedding night, if the woman is a virgin, she may experience a small flow of blood during sexual intercourse. This is normal because the hymen, a fold of mucous membrane partially closing the vagina, is broken. This has become to some, that which forms a blood covenant for their marriage. What about couples where the young ladies have already experienced a flow from their hymen broken before marriage?

This could have happened while participating in strenuous sports events or other activities. Or they could have lost their virginity before marriage engaging in pre-marital relations or possibly being molested or abused.

What about women who have entered into a subsequent marriage? Are these marriages not protected by a blood covenant once the vows have been exchanged? Of course, they are! As shown above, *the marriage covenant, which is also a blood covenant between a man and a woman, was formed for all future marriages in the Lord.*

Furthermore, the marriage is consummated by the wedding vows and not necessarily by an act of sexual union, Malachi 2:14 AMP. Although to many the union is the "final thing" to seal a marriage.

A woman changing her name to her husband's name was a part of the marriage covenant. When God formed Adam's wife, they were both called Adam and it was Adam who renamed his wife "Eve," Genesis 3:20. Eve, which means life spring, because she was the mother of all the living. He also called his wife "wo-man," Genesis 2:23, recognizing her as the counter-part of the male man.

When God made a covenant with people, He often changed their names so they would be called by that which He declared for their destiny. For example, Abram which means "exalted father" was changed to Abraham which now means the father of many nations. He became the father of a multitude, Genesis 17:5.

Jacob was changed to Israel, who became the father of twelve sons who then became the twelve tribes of Israel. Once a couple marries and the wife acquires her husband's name, that is significant in declaring the household which she has become a part of.

Furthermore, **God called her a "helper meet"** (in the KJV she is called a "help meet"). *A help meet is a married woman who is a confidante, encourager, an inward strength, her husband's helper, a comforter and an aid suitable for him. She is someone who is sent by God to help him fulfill his purpose and vision while on this earth. The "helper" does not mean* *inferior but describes a "function" and not "worth."* It can and does include more than birthing children and managing a home according to the Word of God (Proverbs 31:10-31; Ps 68:11; Esther 4:14; and so on).

These are *very important* functions but they are not the only functions God purposed as a woman's part in being her husband's helper. The helper is not there to do it alone but is required to help and participate with the husband. She may also be a woman who has an assignment or mandate from God to fulfill. Hence, God gives everyone a purpose before they enter their mother's womb.

As we know, Holy Spirit (the Third Person of the Godhead) is also called a "Helper" and Jesus also refers to Himself as a "Helper." As a helper, the woman is in good company and is equipped and anointed by God to help her husband. A willingness to help others in a loving manner is the very thing God loves and desires of all His children.

In John 14:16, Jesus is Speaking about Himself and Holy Spirit,

> I will ask the Father, and He will give you *another* Comforter (Counselor, *Helper,* Intercessor, Advocate, Strengthener and Standby), that He may remain with you forever… (Emphasis added.)

A Woman is Her Husband's Help Meet, Genesis 2:18,

> Now the Lord God said, It is not good (sufficient, satisfactory) that the man should be alone; I will make him a helper meet (suitable, adapted, complementary) for him.

Marriage is for People who Have a Covenant with God

Why? God is a part of their marriage covenant. The couple can go to the same Living God and have a relationship, fellowship, receive instructions and any help they may need in any area where it is needed to maintain their marriage and much more.

When they have a need or a situation they cannot remedy, their partner in the marriage covenant has the ability to do so if their hearts are willing to do things God's way. And as a result, they can be an example for others of how *good* God is! He alone is their Source, Wisdom and Way-maker.

When we are equally yoked with the right person and humble enough to follow God's instructions, any marriage can stand the test. From the beginning marriage was intended for a *lifetime, it is still so today and what made it work then is powerful enough to cause it to work today.*

When a man and woman exchange their wedding vows (oath) before God which are repeated before an officiant and witnesses, who are generally family and friends, *they seal and establish a sacred lifetime covenant with one another and with God.*

God takes the wedding covenant seriously even when certain people do not. Wedding vows are a promise to love, honor, respect, cherish and much more. The Lord expects us to fulfill our vows or make a great attempt at fulfilling them, to say the very least. Whatever the Lord asks of someone He has equipped them to do it. The key is to know Him and to know His will in a certain matter. Once that is accomplished, following His instructions to cause something to work will be easier.

However, in a marriage covenant, you are dealing with two people who both have a "free will." One cannot make the other do anything against their free will without causing damage to the relationship. With that in mind, how would these two separate individuals who have been supernaturally joined by the Spirit of God and are now *one* in God's eyes become *one* in the natural? God will help them make it happen as along as He is the head in *their* marriage covenant with Him.

Chapter 7

Suggestions for a
Strong, Successful Marriage

- *When God is first,* He becomes the center of your marriage, your home and your joy. As a result, your household will have knowledge of where and how to acquire the resources that are meaningful for your family to flourish. Resources such as: love, strength, peace, hope, wisdom, joy, healing, faith, provision, self-esteem, security, justice, promotion and more will add tremendously to your marriage. They will know not to put their hope for these things in *man,* whether it is their spouse, parent, sibling, employer or someone else. They should only trust the One who can truly give them these things by His Grace and power, because of their willingness to acknowledge, praise and keep Him first in their lives.

- *Maintain Godly principles found in His Word* regarding marriage and all other areas relevant to everyday life. This will help to *keep God first* in your relationship and enhance your lifestyle. For example, in Ephesians 5:21 NIV it says, *"Submit* to one another out of reverence for Christ" The Amplified Bible says, *"Be subject* to one another out of reverence for Christ (the Messiah, the Anointed One)." Therefore, to submit and to be subject basically is to give honor and respect to those delegated authorities God has placed in our lives. However, when an authoritative figure (an individual, a party, a government, a state, a city, etc.) is not submitting themselves to the will of God, then and only then are you at liberty to rebel against their authority and go with the Word of God. **The Most High God is the final authority** and the One that is given the highest honor and respect. Reason being, He is God. He is the High Priest of all homes that received His sacrifice and *He is the only One Who can back-up His Word!*

- *A successful marriage requires being sensitive to the leading of the Holy Spirit* (being sensitive to what is in your heart for the good of the relationship). This is needed to receive God's instructions for guidance and His timing to carry it out in order to receive breakthroughs and deliverance. *To walk (live) with God is to stay in step with His Holy Spirit.* In other words, continue to flow with Him as He continues to lead you. One reason this is important is because *people change over time and some grow together, whereas others grow apart.* Even though they are both growing, one may grow faster than the other or they may grow in two entirely different directions. For example, one could experience spiritual growth by being influenced by the Word of God and their spouse influenced more so about worldly matters and opinions of men. If they are to remain in agreement and like-minded thinking they will both need to receive growth from the same source.

- *Wisdom and Revelation Knowledge are keys that will empower you* in the proper handling of whatever arises. Using the "instruction manual" is going to the source which can only benefit and enhance the proper and full use of what is being used, operated or studied. Our instruction manual is the Holy Bible and from it we can:

Get Wisdom and *Understanding;* Proverbs 4:7-13 says,

The beginning of Wisdom is: get Wisdom (skillful and godly Wisdom)! **[For skillful and Godly Wisdom is the principal thing.]** And with all you have gotten, get *understanding* (discernment, comprehension, and interpretation). Prize

Wisdom highly and exalt her, and she will exalt and promote you; *she will bring you to honor when you embrace her.* She shall give to your head a wreath of gracefulness; a crown of beauty and glory will she deliver to you. Hear, O My son, and receive My sayings, and the years of your life shall be many. I have taught you in the way of skillful and godly Wisdom [which is comprehensive insight into the ways and purposes of God]; I have led you in paths of uprightness. When you walk, your steps shall not be hampered [your path will be clear and open]; and when you run, you shall not stumble. *Take firm hold of instruction, do not let go; guard her, for she is your life.*

Proverbs 2:2-8 NLT says,

"My child, listen to Me and treasure My instructions. *Tune your ears to wisdom and concentrate on understanding.* Cry out for insight and understanding. Search for them as you would for lost money or hidden treasure. Then you will understand what it means to fear the Lord, and you will gain knowledge of God. For the Lord grants wisdom! From His mouth come knowledge and understanding. *He grants a treasure of good sense to the godly. He is their shield, protecting those who walk with integrity.* He guards the paths of justice and protects those who are faithful to Him."

- Through wisdom we understand it was *God's design a man should not be alone but to have a "Helpmate"* and thus God introduced man to woman, a husband to his wife, Genesis 2:18-22.

- *Husbands and wives would remove their guards when speaking to each other if they truly better understood their differences.* Behind some of the things men perceive as a wife nagging or the wife being insulted because the husband rejects her thoughts, wisdom, insight on matters that would have made a difference for the better, had she been heard. If the couple understood she is not nagging to nag, or reminding you just for the sake of it, but she has a built-in desire given to her by God to be a "helpmate" to honestly help. *She was created with a natural need to secure, protect, correct, and give advice.* On the other hand, *most men do not see themselves as needing a helper. Even though God said He did and gave him someone to bring the help where the man is lacking.* Men view themselves as the ones who solve problems, fix things and are independent operators. They do not feel they need "extra" from their wife. They do not want any advice, warnings, or second opinions. As a result, they miss great blessings and opportunities because the "right" wife, the one God sent, is on assignment from the Lord to help her husband fulfill the vision God gave him. Women are given godly wisdom for some things men do not have wisdom for. Women think in detail and they use both sides of their brains far more frequently than men do. God will impart to her supernaturally the wisdom to turn a house into a home and make things pleasant for the entire family; run a business; have a career and the like. But He will also give her wisdom to be still if it is not appreciated or her gifts are rejected by her husband. A true husband is given wisdom to lead his family with the love of Christ. He thinks more in general terms and does all sorts of things women do not usually do that will also benefit the entire family. If both really knew their individual value and why they express themselves the way they do to one another they would appreciate each other's gifts and talents and realize it was because they are different. When they bring their differences to the table they will find many of the places where they struggled separately that together they solve and progress in victory.

- *Celebrate each other's differences.* You are not together to compete with one another but complement and enhance your efforts as a married couple. To be there for each other, giving support in the areas where one is weak and the other is strong. *As you function this way in love* you will have the opportunity to not only have a successful marriage but to be a light and comfort to another couple who may be struggling in their marriage.

- *Making a commitment to walk in love* will require that you do something. Saying the words are wonderful but action speaks louder than words to the receiver. Reaching out to participate in a date night, breakfast or lunch with your spouse; planning time when you can discuss issues of the household or other pressing things. Planning times to take walks and discuss lighter matters; watching sports with your husband on occasion or he watching a movie with his wife and the like; as well as reaching out or helping each other with different projects will require some type of sacrifice on your part and shows commitment and love. These and other couple activities contribute to a stronger relationship and open communication. Your time, altering your plans to be there for your spouse is a part of marriage. Do all with a kind heart and unto the Lord. What you do for someone in secret God rewards in the open. You may not be doing it for a reward but when you do something for someone else it plants a seed for God to do something for you or your household wherever there is a need. This is how the Kingdom of God operates. However, if your heart is not right and you are only going through the motions and really could care less about your spouse's needs and you are looking only to be seen, know this, God sees the heart and whatever you are doing is all the reward you will receive.

- *Two people the Lord brings together will have a vision or a dream specifically given for them to accomplish together as a part of the purpose for their lives and for their marriage.* This vision or dream will usually be larger than what the both of them can accomplish without God's assistance. They will have to live by faith and follow His instructions and receive His help for it to come to pass. This dream or vision will be a tremendous reminder of how important it is for them to come in agreement and to stay together because one cannot do this without the other. They will know and realize this is larger than the two of them and if they were to separate or divorce it will affect more lives than their family. Therefore, the reason you are together is bigger than having your personal marriage, family, home, business and all the things you have accumulated together. This vision or dream can become a reality because you know that it did not originate from yourselves but instead was given by The Creative Mind Who holds all Power. By divine inspiration and revelation one concludes if He began this work in us, He can finish it. As long as you are willing to see it come to pass, humble yourself and rely on the Master's Plan then you set yourself up to win and take the prize. This prize will affect others and in turn be so gratifying and fulfilling because you dared to step into your destiny and be a part of the overall plan of an awesome God.

- As we express our love towards our spouse, *the choice of our words is extremely important* in order to accomplish this. Words are very powerful and an effective tool. As we are able to express our feelings, love and appreciation for our spouse through our words they become a blessing to our spouse. *Words can be used to honor a person when we realize all people have God-given worth* and assets. Therefore, something nice *can* be said about anyone.

- Words are not some empty sound that just float out of our mouths. ***Words are "spirit," they are alive and have power.*** *They can give life or if we use them improperly with our tongues they can bring death,* Proverbs 18:21. God said He is a *Spirit* in John 4:2. We are made in His likeness, a spirit being that has a soul and lives in a body, I Thess. 5:23. When God communicates with us, He speaks directly to our spirit man through His Holy Spirit. He does not speak to our bodies or our soul (mind, will and emotions). He speaks to our spirit and our spirit conveys it to our mind which controls our body through our brain. Therefore, when we speak to our spouse, our spirit is speaking to their spirit (which is the real person). *The choice of our words will bring life or death, build them up or tear them down, literally, because the words are alive and have power.* So, speak uplifting words and bless your spouse, Hebrews 4:12.

- Some of the most successful and joyous couples say, ***"I love you"*** *to each other.* It sets the atmosphere to continuously build on a solid foundation. Since their words have power, they are *releasing or sending* love to that person every time they speak those words into the atmosphere because those are *godly words.* At the same time, *you are instructing Holy Spirit to* *fill you with a love towards your spouse when you say the words, I love you.* Why does this happen? Because the words you spoke were in line with God's will, therefore, it is set to come to pass. You are also *strengthening the commitment* you have for one another when you speak Godly words. No one can have a true and lasting love for their spouse without making a strong commitment in words and in deeds.

- ***When a wife is too harsh in communicating*** with her husband it says to him, you do not honor and respect me and I do not believe in you. When the tone is wrong he cannot receive from her. ***When a husband speaks harsh to his wife*** it can convey he does not care about her as a person. Both of these conclusions are out of proportion but none the less *it opens a door and gives Satan a foothold to work with.* Speak the truth in love when at all possible. Self-control and taking a few deep breaths while thinking through the moment will help to manage it in a better way. We cannot help how we feel but we can help how we behave and respond. Do not allow your emotions to control you to the point your tongue is out of control, James 3:8-10; James 4:11-12. Also try to capture your thoughts and submit them to Christ before things get out of hand, 2 Corinthians 10:4-5. Ask God to put a guard on your mouth so you will not sin with your tongue, Ps. 141:3. The Word says, to let the words of your mouth and the mediations of your heart be acceptable in the sight of God, Ps. 19:14. Ask the Lord to help you tame your tongue and think about your words before you speak. We should be quick to hear, slow to speak and slow to take offense, James 1:19. *We can control what comes out of our mouths with the help of Holy Spirit.*

* The Bible says, **God's words will not return to Him void,** Isaiah 55:11. Therefore, if we speak His Words "over" *or* "to" our spouse those *words will produce a harvest* by accomplishing what they were sent to do. Things will come to pass when they manifest as a result of the words we have spoken, whether they are God-given words or negative words. Why? *Words bring us into our destiny.* Someone once said, "watch your **thoughts** because they become **words**; choose your words because they become **action**; understand your actions because they become **habits**; study your habits because they become your **character**; develop your character because it becomes your **destiny**." Your gifts and talents can open a door of opportunity but your character is what will sustain you once you are there. It all starts with speaking out our

thoughts. The first action taken is *releasing* the *words* because thoughts do not produce anything so we have the option of casting down the wrong thoughts and only speaking the correct ones. Therefore, it is your choice as to whether they are words that will bring life or words that will bring death, it is up to you, Proverbs 18:21.

- *Attentive listening encourages and blesses the speaker.* Even if some women go on and on about the same subject, if a husband can just listen and acknowledge she is speaking by making a *remark* every now and then will allow her to express herself fully. For example, by saying "really," "wow," "yes dear" or any sound to let her know he is still making an effort to listen to her as she attempts to express or vent something she needs to release. He does not always need to "fix" something but just have a "listening ear." She will eventually move on to another topic having fulfilled this desire to express what was in her heart. *BUT, if she continues with the same subject far beyond reason, she may require more than just a listening ear.* Therefore, he may gently suggest a third party, like a good friend or mother, or father, or Christian counselor to listen and to get their opinion. Sometimes the person speaking repeatedly about an issue either needs an answer, a need met, healing in a certain area or to forgive. Therefore, they may need to seek another reliable ear before they wear their spouse out.

- *Communication is a skill* which develops with practice and encouragement from one another. Prayer is extremely important to keep the interpretation of what is actually being said or intended, from not becoming distorted or misinterpreted by the hearer. When you ask the Holy Spirit to help you understand or give you clarity in understanding your spouse, while in prayer, from time to time say, *"In the name of Jesus, I plead the blood of Jesus over my ears and the ears of my spouse."* You will find it will be easier to get the true meaning of what you are actually saying to one another and hopefully you will receive this divine intervention and spiritual weapon before someone arrives at the wrong conclusion or becomes offended.

- *When the words spoken are constantly negative* then once released from our mouths into the atmosphere those words will *not* be used by the Holy Spirit. Angelic forces will not produce a harvest from negative ungodly words. Instead, evil demonic forces will pick those words up and will bring those words to pass if you have not repented and placed those negative words under the Blood of Jesus to stop them from harvesting. Therefore, speak Godly, uplifting positive words to prevent receiving a negative harvest.

- *Remember there is an assignment against marriages from Satan* who hates marriage because he hates God. He will do all he can to cause confusion and misunderstandings by sending negative thoughts to one or both partners in order to keep strife in the home. Therefore, think before you speak. You do not have to say *everything* that comes to your mind especially if it is negative. *Ask God to guard your mouth.* "Set a guard, O Lord, before my mouth; keep watch at the door of my lips," Psalms 141:3 or "Take control of what I say, O Lord, and keep my lips sealed," Psalms 141:3 NLT. If you feel you must say something, then ask the Holy Spirit to help you word it so it will be received well. The Holy Spirit will help you develop and exercise control over your language, Proverbs 21:23; Proverbs 18:21; Proverbs 15:1; Proverbs 16:24; James 1:19; and Proverbs 19:14.

Colossians 4:6 tells us,

> Let your speech at all times be gracious (pleasant and winsome), seasoned [as it were] with salt, [so that you may never be at a loss] to know how you ought to answer anyone [who puts a question to you].

Ephesians 4:29-32 tells us,

> Let no foul *or* polluting language, *nor* evil word *nor* unwholesome *or* worthless talk [ever] come out of your mouth, but only such [speech] as is good *and* beneficial to the spiritual progress of others, as is fitting to the need *and* the occasion, that it may be a blessing *and* give grace (God's favor) to those who hear it. And do not grieve the Holy Spirit of God... Let all bitterness *and* indignation *and* wrath (passion, rage, bad temper) and resentment (anger, animosity) and quarreling (brawling, clamor, contention) and slander (evil-speaking, abusive or blasphemous language) be banished from you, with all malice (spite, ill will, or baseness of any kind). And become useful *and* helpful *and* kind to one another, tenderhearted (compassionate, understanding, loving-

hearted), forgiving one another [readily and freely], as God in Christ forgave you.

* *A lack of communication* is one of the main reasons people separate or divorce. In most cases, it can be resolved with proper skills in communicating which involves *listening and speaking in the right tones* and so forth. In communicating the couple should welcome and be able to discuss any topic, especially those about their marriage, children, work, friends, extended family, finances, their business and so on. Be considerate of the point the other person is making. *Try to discuss one topic at a time.* However, for some who do not wish to communicate but would rather dismiss those things that were really hurtful or dismiss those things needed to be confronted will find it will eventually come out anyway. How it comes out will be the key of whether major or minor damage will be done. When at all possible please realize it is better to talk and release.

* If the person is ***passive-aggressive*** then revenge will usually be with some sort of indirect retaliation at a time the other person least expects it. They refuse to confront because of fear, possible insecurities or just not wanting to

deal with the other person's response. But to wait for an opportune time to "get them back" is revengeful, it demonstrates unforgiveness and bitterness has had space to build up. Remember, the Lord said vengeance is His and He will repay, Romans 12:19. We are to forgive, confront, bless and so forth. The same holds true with the *silent treatment* used to punish the other person with emotional starvation. These things are rooted in unforgiveness with angry unresolved issues. They are only blocking their own blessings because their actions are not godly. These devices are far worse for the person executing them. If they simply would have spoken up at the time they should have and cleared the air and dealt with the situation or the response they may or may not have received, it would have been better for both parties. Confronting a situation offers a chance to resolve and finish it, coming to some type of an agreement and moving on.

- *A major key is to agree to talk, if at all possible, at a time when they are in a relaxed atmosphere. They can also agree to disagree peacefully* and be willing to discuss any disagreements further until they come to some sort of resolution. They should be aware of their voice, facial expressions and keeping in mind to show their spouse respect whether they agree or not. I would like to add if the atmosphere does change and barriers go up such as offense, pride, anger or guilt, making it difficult to express personal feelings or emotions, then it would be better to terminate the conversation. Do not allow it to turn into an argument or even an attack on the other person by speaking words that may be regretted later. If the both of you can, pray and thank God you got this far and ask Him to help you reach an understanding. Then, in agreement, set up a continuation for the discussion at a specified date, time and place. Maybe somewhere casual or relaxing, where you can finish and hopefully develop a strategy that will resolve the issues at hand.

- It is always better to at least try to communicate. *Work it out even if a **professional third party** or someone you really trust* has to be brought to the table. A marriage is worth saving, restoring and renewing. Try seeking outside help from a qualified Christian counselor, coach or someone knowledgeable you can trust. Realize a mediator can bring a different perspective, be more objective since they are not emotionally involved and can hear and see more clearly on how to reach a successful resolution to your problem, Proverbs 15:22.

- *Proper management of finances* is very important in maintaining a strong marriage. There should always be open communication and both spouses should know and have access to the "Biblical Spending Plan" your household uses. Joint accounts are also advised to block Satan from working with deceiving devices between the couple. (See *God's Way and Finances* for biblical suggestions for managing finances.)

- *Selfishness* is at the heart of almost every marital problem so practice giving and helping to take the attention off of yourself. Try thinking about others first. Ask God how you can be a blessing to someone else especially your spouse, children, extended family, friends and neighbors. Jesus taught a successful marriage was not about selfishness but about selflessness. *It is about giving, sharing and being transparent in order to bind together.* Anything less would only be a prescription for a disaster to occur.

- *Strive to keep strife out of your marriage and entire household. It is a killer.* It will rob you of your peace, joy, faith, miracles and any power you have as a couple especially if you are praying together. Strife is bickering, arguing, heated disagreements or an angry undercurrent. It opens a door to every evil and vile practice. The enemy will come in and use devices against your marriage to do as much damage as possible to your relationship. Strife is dangerous, destructive and will spread rapidly unless it is confronted and stopped. Since all couples argue from time to time, I suggest being very watchful and monitor the strife (the *constant* bickering and arguing). Instead, pray, use wisdom, get constructive advice from outside mentors, books, tools and other methods for making your point. *A wife does not need to brow beat or nag but simply with a calm tone in her voice state her need and then trust God to work with her husband's heart or hers.* This will help to control or stop the strife from becoming more frequent, 2 Timothy 2:23-24, Isaiah 32:18; Proverbs 16:32; Proverbs 17:14; and James 1:19-20, James 3:16. (See *God's Way and Spiritual Warfare* for information regarding marriage, praying effective prayers for your marriage and more.)

- Married people should spend as much **leisure time together** as possible. Date nights, date breakfasts or date lunches, once or twice a week, are always nice. They remind a couple they are a romantic couple *before* they are parents, business partners or before any other demand is placed on their relationship. On these dates or just at home, spending leisure time together, going for walks, exercising together, watching a movie or having a snack together, remember to keep the conversation "light." This is so you will not discourage one another from spending these healthy, joyful times together in fear of constant reminders of heavy responsibilities. *There should be other times set aside to pray together as well as set times to discuss finances, management of your home, family, business* and so forth.

- Couples with strong marriages should also recognize even though they are one in the spirit and flesh (like-mindedness) they are still **different genders, two different individuals.** They need to allow each other time to express themselves while they are developing common bonds and shared interest. Doing things of interest without their spouse such as having lunch with extended family members or friends, enjoying sports events, shopping, taking a class and so forth will help to strengthen their union. *It will also assist in keeping balance in the relationship which is very important.*

- There is an old saying that says, "The grass is always greener on the other side of the fence." However, if you water your own grass it will be green too. In other words, if you take care of your relationship by doing things *God's Way*, decent and in order, your marriage will flourish beyond your expectations.

Marriage can be fulfilling and challenging at the same time. However, marriage is well worth it. There are many, many wonderful benefits a married couple can enjoy. To name a few: having the privilege to love someone else and be loved, having companionship, comfort, contentment, security, stability, fun, excitement, being special in someone else's life and being pleasing to God.

You can enjoy one another without trying to change anything about the person. When exercising unconditional love, you can choose to accept them and they accept you just the way you are. You can be committed in a meaningful relationship that has vision, goals and dreams going in the same direction in life.

You will experience peace being with a mate that is not competing with you, jealous of you or what you were purposed for in life. Instead share as you assist one another in becoming all you were meant to be in Christ.

None of the above would be possible if we did not consistently have God first in our lives. When He is first, the love and trust is there and all the rest of it just lines up. When there are difficult times, and we all have them, we do not have to rely on ourselves or even each other to come through because we realize we have a Covenant Partner and a loving Savior Who truly loves us and wants the best for us. He will change hearts and make a way where there seems to be none.

As we continue to move forward, He will be with us every step of the way. It is all about us making a decision to do the right thing, trusting God to let His grace and mercy do what needs to be done in order to cause our lives to be empowered and blessed the way He desires and purposed.

And in turn we bless Him by blessing others!

APPENDIX A

A Prayer for Salvation and the Infilling of the Holy Spirit

If you are not a Born-again Christian with the Infilling (Baptism) of the Holy Spirit, or you are a Christian Believer and would like to rededicate your life to Jesus, say the following prayer. Afterwards, tell someone of the decision you have made regarding the Good News!

Dear Heavenly Father,

I come to You now, just as I am in the name of Jesus. Your Word says, "…Whosoever shall call on the name of the Lord shall be saved," Acts 2:21. And it says, "that if you confess with your mouth Jesus is Lord and believe in your heart that God raised Him from the dead, you will be saved" according to Romans 10:9.

I believe and confess now that Jesus (Yeshua) is the Son of God and He is alive today. I receive Him as my personal Lord and Savior. I ask for forgiveness and repent of my past sins and I choose to forgive others for their trespasses. Thank You Father God that Your Son has set me free from eternal darkness. I now declare that I am redeemed, I am healed, I am blessed, and I am whole. Therefore, I now have a renewed, abundant and confident life in Christ Jesus, the Messiah.

Father God, You said my Salvation would be the result of Your Holy Spirit giving me new birth by coming to live in me Romans 8:9, 11. So I ask You now for the Infilling of Your Holy Spirit as you have promised. Thank You for the gift to speak in other tongues, my spiritual prayer language that is unknown to man but known to God according to Acts 2:4 and I Corinthians 14:2. Now I bind the strong man that was sent to rob me and I plead the Blood of Jesus over my mind and mouth as I now release from my spirit my supernatural prayer language in Jesus' Mighty name. Amen! Give God Thanks!

The above Prayer is based on Romans 10:9-10 NKJV which says,

"That if you confess with your mouth the Lord Jesus and believe in your heart that God has raised Him from the dead, you will be saved. For with the heart one believes unto righteousness, and with the mouth confession is made unto salvation."

I John 2:2, 12 AMP says,

"And He [that same Jesus Himself] is the propitiation (the atoning sacrifice) for our sins, and not for ours alone but also for [the sins of] the whole world. ...*because for His name's sake your sins are forgiven [pardoned through His name and on account of confessing His name].*"

"Justified" – We are as if we never sinned! We are declared righteous, acceptable to God because of the Finished Work at the Cross where Jesus took our sins and gave us His Righteousness because in Him we have redemption through the blood! Hallelujah for a God Who Saves, Ephesians 1:7, Acts 4:12.

Salvation Scriptures:

Romans 10:9-10; John 3:14-17; John 5:24; Acts 2:21; John 10:9-18; John 6:44-51; Ps 51:5; Acts 4:12; Mt. 1:21; I Peter 1:23; Ro. 3:23; I John 1:9; Acts 3:13-26; 2 Cor. 4:4; Eph. 2:8-10; Ro. 6:4; Ro. 5:8; John 14:6; I John 4:9-10; John 3:3-6,15-16; Mt. 12:40; I Cor. 15:22; Acts 10: 40; Acts 16:31; Col. 2:6-7, Acts 15:11

Infilling of the Holy Spirit Scriptures:

Acts 2:1-4; I Co. 2:4-5; Acts 10:44-48; Acts l: 5, 8; Acts 2: 39; Acts 11:16; John 4:23-24; Romans 8:6-17, 26-27; John 1:33; Eph. 6:18; Jude 1:20; I Cor. 2:14; I Cor. 6:19-20; I Cor. 14:2-15, 18; Luke 11:13; Ezekiel 11:19; I Cor. 12:7-11; Eph. 5:18; John 16:13; Gal. 5:22-23; Isaiah 11:2-3; Romans 6:1-11

APPENDIX B

What is Salvation?

God so greatly loved the world that He gave His one and only Son, that whoever believes in Him shall not perish but have eternal life, John 3:16. Because of what Jesus did on the cross, a way was made for people (Jew and Gentile) to be reconciled back to Father God through Salvation. This brought forth the "Believer," which is the One New Man, Eph. 2:14-16. "And there is salvation in *and* through no one else, *for there is no other name under heaven given among men by and in which we must be saved,"* Acts 4:12, the Amplified Bible.

In John 3:14-17 Jesus explains,

> And just as Moses lifted up the serpent in the desert [on a pole], so must [so it is necessary that] the Son of Man be lifted up [on the cross], In order that everyone who believes in Him [who cleaves to Him, trusts Him, and relies on Him] *may not perish, but* have eternal life *and* [actually] live forever! For God so greatly loved *and* dearly prized the world that He [even] gave up His only begotten (unique) Son, so that whoever believes in (trusts in, clings to, relies on) Him shall not perish (come to destruction, be lost)

but have eternal (everlasting) life. For God did not send the Son into the world in order to judge (reject, to condemn, to pass sentence on) the world, but that the world might find salvation *and* be made safe *and* sound through Him.

When you receive Yeshua HaMashiach, (Jesus the Christ, the Messiah, the Anointed One) you are saved. "For it is by free grace (God's unmerited favor) that you are saved (delivered from judgment *and* made partakers of Christ's salvation) through [your] faith. And this [salvation] is not of yourselves [of your own doing, it came not through your own striving], but it is the gift of God," Eph. 2:8.

The word "saved" is the English word for the Greek word "Sozo" which was used to define the Hebrew word "Shalom." "To be saved is defined as: to deliver or protect – heal, preserve, save, do well, be (make) whole," (Strong's Concordance).

A personal relationship with God is included. The Holy Spirit is with you, inside of you and will communicate with your spirit. You are also entitled to good health, preservation, protection, provision, prosperity, favor, peace, good relationships, purpose, safety, deliverance, authority, soundness, spiritual gifts, strength, mercy, guidance, angelic help, increase and more! In other words, wholeness (Shalom).

Furthermore, the English word **"save"** is used in the New Testament to define the Hebrew word **"Shalom."** Another term used to describe "save" is **born-again.** Jesus said "unless one is born again, he cannot see the kingdom of God," John 3:1-6; I Peter 1:3.

The name Yeshua (Jesus) means Savior or Salvation. Salvation makes you whole as you grow in Messiah, Matt. 1:21. *Therefore, Yeshua restores "Shalom" making you whole - nothing broken and nothing missing.* He is the Pioneer of your Salvation, Heb. 2:10.

Jesus is also referred to as the Prince of Peace (Sar Shalom) and "Peace comes to you because you are whole!" Hebrews 13:20-21 NKJV says, "Now may the God of peace who brought up our Lord Jesus from the dead, that great Shepherd of the sheep, through the blood of the everlasting covenant, make you complete in every good work to do His will, working in you what is well pleasing in His sight, through Jesus Christ, to whom *be* glory forever and ever. Amen."

To be saved is to have Salvation (Yeshua). Everything you will ever need is found in salvation. *The most important thing about receiving salvation is in Christ you become a new creation; salvation comes with the New Covenant and salvation includes eternal life,* 2 Cor. 5:17; Jeremiah 31:31-33; Matthew 26:26-29; Luke 22:20; Romans

2:28-29; Galatians 2:16 and Galatians 3:7-14; 26-29; John 3:16, 36.

Salvation prevents anyone from perishing for their sin for eternity in outer darkness. Instead of death they will receive eternal life, John 3:36. In addition, while still on earth the Believer receives "The Blessing" which encompasses all the blessings from the Lord in the Kingdom of God.

Because we accepted the Father's sacrifice, Jesus/Yeshua, the Father *adopted us* into His Family (the Family of God, the One New Man).

Romans 8:15 says,

> For [the Spirit which] you have now received [is] not a spirit of slavery to put you once more in bondage to fear, but you have received the Spirit of adoption [the Spirit producing sonship] in [the bliss of] which we cry, Abba (Father)! Father!

The word adoption basically means a person is brought into the Family of God even though they were previously without any covenant with Him. Like all of us who are born-again (John 3:1-3) we were sinners and separated from God, but God in His mercy and grace redeemed us, purchased us and brought us into His presence. In His presence once again, this time through the blood of His only beloved Son, Jesus.

Once saved we are adopted by God, Who chose and received us as His own. What an honor, for Almighty God to choose us and then pour His love on each and every one of us. As Christian Believers in Christ Messiah, the Anointed One.

We are now eternally part of His family. His Spirit dwells in our spirit man and communes with us. Because of the adoption we become heirs of God and joint heirs with His Son, Jesus the Christ (Yeshua HaMashiach), Romans 8:17.

So how does one receive their salvation? Romans 10:9-10 NKJV, "that if you confess with your mouth the Lord Jesus and believe in your heart that God has raised Him from the dead, you will be saved. For with the heart one believes unto righteousness, and with the mouth confession is made unto salvation."

NOTES

Chapter One:
The Origin of Marriage

1. Disciple's Study Bible, NIV Footnote. Nashville: Holman Bible Publisher, 1988
2. The New Unger's Bible Dictionary. Chicago: Moody Press, 1988

Chapter Two:
The Marriage Protocol, Early to Modern Times

1. Perry Stone, *The Ancient Jewish Wedding A Revelation on the Rapture; The Mystery of the Four Passover Cups.*
www.perrystone.org/store/index.php/dvds-all/dvds/dv094: DVD DV094
2. Disciple's Study Bible, NIV Nashville: Holman Bible Publishers, 1988
3. Zola Levitt, of Levitt Letter: January 2006 article, *Our Marriage in Heaven*, Dallas: Levitt Letter article condensed by his son Aaron, January 2018

Chapter Three:
The Reasons for Marriage

1. The New Unger's Bible Dictionary. Chicago: Moody Press, 1988

Chapter Six:
The Marriage Covenant

1. The New Unger's Bible Dictionary. Chicago: Moody Press, 1988
2. ibid
3. Disciple's Study Bible, NIV Nashville: Holman Bible Publisher, 1988
4. Vine's Complete Expository Dictionary with Topical Index. Nashville: Thomas Nelson Publisher, 1984, 1996
5. ibid
6. ibid
7. ibid
8. ibid
9. Disciple's Study Bible, NIV Nashville: Holman Bible Publisher, 1988
10. ibid
11. The New Unger's Bible Dictionary. Chicago: Moody Press, 1988
12. H. A. Maxwell Whyte, The Power of the Blood. New Kensington: Whitaker House, 1973
13. ibid
14. ibid
15. The New Unger's Bible Dictionary. Chicago: Moody Press, 1988
16. ibid
17. Disciple's Study Bible, NIV Nashville: Holman Bible Publisher, 1988
18. ibid

19. The New Unger's Bible Dictionary. Chicago: Moody Press, 1988

About the Author

Audrey L. Dickey, D.Min., Ph.D. is an apostle, prophetic voice, author and conference speaker. She ministers the Word and counsels prophetically to advance the fivefold ministry in the Kingdom of God. Her books include spiritual warfare strategies and tools for marriages, families, finances, everyday life experiences and Kingdom business. Since her youth she has seen signs and wonders, healings and prophecies come to pass through the power of God. Dr. Audrey holds a Doctor of Philosophy in Religious Studies and a Doctor of Ministry with emphasis in Biblical Counseling from FICU in California. She is also a member of the American Association of Christian Counselors (AACC). She along with her husband, Robert L. Dickey, Ph.D. received a vision to establish an international apostolic, prophetic ministry. They are the founders and CEO's of Christian Love Glory International Center as well as the founders and apostles of Christian Love Fellowship Church, Inc. This Fivefold multi-cultural ministry includes covenant restoration of the One New Man and will oversee designated marketplace businesses. Drs. Robert and Audrey Dickey have five children and make their home in Los Angeles, California.

To Contact the Author:
Dr. Audrey L. Dickey
P. O. 48288
Los Angeles, CA 90048
www.robertandaudreydickeyministries.org

Other Books by Audrey L. Dickey

<u>GOD'S WAY SERIES</u>

God's Way and Family

God's Way and the Blended Family

God's Way and Finances

God's Way and Knowing the King

God's Way and Divorce

God's Way and Spiritual Warfare